REVEALED

A ONCE-A-WEEK READING TO UNDERSTAND RACISM, PREJUDICE, AND BIAS

TAMARA LUCAS COPELAND

Revealed

A Once-A-Week Reading to Understand Racism, Prejudice, and Bias

ISBN 979-8-9860859-4-4

Published in the United States of America by Inspire, an Adducent nonfiction imprint.

Adducent, Inc.
Jacksonville, Florida
www.AdducentCreative.com

Cover Art by Rayhart: www.Rayhart.com

CONTENTS

About the Cover Artist

RAYHART

WWW.RAYHART.COM

The artist describes his style as 'open, somewhat abstract, somewhat surreal.'

"Through art, I wage war within myself for the rewards of peace. I adore each painting like a mother's first glimpse at her newborn. In short, I paint to allow for creation." —Rayhart

"When you know better, do better."

—Maya Angelou

FOREWORD

That we are living at a time of profound racial tension and separation is no secret to any sentient being. The Black Lives Matter movement for social justice triggered by the murder of George Floyd seemed to foreshadow a new possibility for racial healing in the United States as thousands took to the streets, even in the face of the COVID pandemic, to call for racial equity and accountability. And yet, within weeks, a backlash against teaching about race resulted in the banning (and occasional burning) of books, firing of teachers, rewriting of school curricula to reflect a white-centric agenda, and a general dismissal by a significant part of our country of the concept of racial healing based on the acknowledgment of the true history of our country.

As quickly as a new possibility for healing emerged, the same old question replaced it: Can we ever learn to talk about race constructively as a society? Sadly, the answer still seems to be, "Not yet."

It is in that context that I find Tamara Copeland's book REVEALED to be a breath of fresh air.

This is not a "feel good" book. It is too honest and way too thought-provoking to fit that description. It is a book, however, that can go a long way to helping us understand the scope of the challenge we are facing as individuals and as a society at large.

The form of the book is an incredibly usable, practical, and effective teaching tool. Each of the weekly "reads" is, in and of itself, a lesson in our understanding of the dynamics of race. It calls for us to stop, listen, think, and digest in a way that the modern reader can easily absorb and get meaning from. It gives us not only things to think and learn about but also tools that can practically help us develop our own racial consciousness and find ways to contribute to the larger dialogue on race. And yet, it is the breadth and depth of the substance of the writing that will impact the readers the most.

Speaking from the perspective of an African American woman whose own life has reflected the trials and triumphs of living in a white-dominant world, Copeland's honesty and her willingness to offer deep self-reflection gives us remarkable insight into the very real human impact of our racial discord and, even more importantly, the system that has created and sustained that discord for the entire existence of our country. Copeland shares all of that from her perspective while also engendering deep compassion and empathy for others.

The topics that are covered are a robust collection of real-life issues that individuals and society face as we take on the challenge of understanding the racial dynamics that the Swedish sociologist Gunnar Myrdal referred to as the *American Dilemma*. In a little over 200 pages, Copeland addresses the way race inserts itself into our lives in various ways: Black doctors being disrespected despite their sterling credentials; the inequitable medical and financial impact of the COVID pandemic on the Black community; Colin Kaepernick and the Black Lives Matter protest movement; the deaths of Trayvon Martin and so many other unarmed African Americans; how we deal with statues of Confederate notables; the cultural expressions of culture, hair, etc.; the importance of language and its impact on us, and other similarly important conversations that we are much too reticent, as a society as a whole, to thoughtfully discuss.

These conversations are, oddly, timeless and timebound at the same time, and in her presentation of them, Copeland calls us to understand the history we know and that which we don't. A history so often simultaneously acknowledged and denied, as it seems to serve people's needs to do so. Copeland seems to concurrently speak from the perspective of generations, including the current ones.

Copeland shares her own experience as an accomplished professional African American woman to personalize her writing in a deep and meaningful way. I have to admit to being somewhat biased because I know Copeland's work and the positive community impact she has had for many years, but I would wager that any reader will be deeply impressed by the intelligence, sensitivity, and thoughtfulness she writes with. This is not a book emerging from her own psychic trauma, as so many are, but one that brings a critical level of consciousness to every page and passage.

Copeland reminds us of the power and importance of courage, not only by evoking heroes and sheroes of the past and present (e.g., James Baldwin, Ida B. Wells, Rosa Parks, Kaepernick, Jose Andres, etc.) but by calling us into action to demonstrate our own "profiles in courage."

Every section of the book offers not just polemic but an evidence-based pathway to greater understanding. Sometimes through the questions she poses that take us to a deeper level of inquiry. Sometimes through exercises that she asks us to participate in. Sometimes through providing us with resources that we can utilize to take us to a deeper level of engagement and understanding.

Copeland calls us to really look at and understand, at a profound level, what it means to be an American in the 21st Century regarding the issue of race.

As a white Jewish man who has spent a lifetime fighting for racial justice, I found, and I think every reader will find, this book to be a breath of fresh air. Not easy, but honest. Not simple, but understandable. And, perhaps most importantly, not pessimistic but hopeful. And that is what moved me the most about this valuable little book: it strikes me as a call to hope.

Not hope in the sense of a slogan or in the sense of ungrounded optimism. In fact, Copeland captures hopefulness in a way that was perhaps best described by the Czech poet, playwright, turned activist Vaclav Havel, who said,

The kind of hope I often think about (especially in situations that are particularly hopeless, such as prison) I understand above all as a state of mind, not a state of the world. Either we have hope within us, or we don't; it is a dimension of the soul; it's not essentially dependent on some particular observation of the world or estimate of the situation. Hope is not prognostication. It is an orientation of the spirit, an orientation of the heart; it transcends the world that is immediately experienced and is anchored somewhere beyond its horizons. Hope, in this deep and powerful sense, is not the same as joy that things are going well or willingness to invest in enterprises that are obviously headed for early success, but, rather, an ability to work for something because it is good, not just because it stands a chance to succeed.

Copeland leaves us with hope. Hope that we can keep learning about ourselves, others, and our society. Hope that change is possible. Hope that through our individual and collective efforts, we can make a difference. Hope that a future is possible that is not wedded to the past.

This is not only a book... it is a tool... one that can help us build a better, brighter, more hopeful tomorrow.

—Howard J. Ross

A lifelong social justice advocate considered one of the world's seminal thought leaders on identifying and addressing unconscious bias, he is the author of *ReInventing Diversity: Transforming Organizational Community to Strengthen People, Purpose, and Performance*, the Washington Post best seller, *Everyday Bias: Identifying and Navigating Unconscious Judgments in Our Daily Lives*, and *Our Search for Belonging: How Our Need to Connect is Tearing Us Apart*. His writings have been published by the Harvard Business Review, the Washington Post, the New York Times, Fast Company Magazine, Diversity Women Magazine, Forbes Magazine, Fortune Magazine, and dozens of other publications. He appears monthly on National Public Radio.

INTRODUCTION

Hello,

I'm excited that you chose to read REVEALED. It means you are committed to being a lifelong learner about racial inequity, equity, and justice. What better time to start than the beginning of the year.

Some background to offer context for my writing and perspective:

I'm Tamara Lucas Copeland, a Black woman, an only child, raised and educated in the South. I was raised in a two-parent family. My Mom, educated as a Registered Nurse, became a stay-at-home mom after my birth. She was passionate about her family and exploring her family's genealogy. My Dad was a small business owner and a real estate broker. He valued financial success but was most concerned about having a quality life and providing it for his family. I lived a middle-class life in what, at the time, would have been called a "Leave It to Beaver" segregated community. I attended an all-Black elementary school until the 6th grade when I was allowed to enter the newly integrated public school system in Richmond, Virginia, my hometown. College was a predominantly white school, the College of William and Mary, followed by grad school at an urban university, Virginia Commonwealth University. I worked in public policy focused on policy benefiting children and families for most of my adult life, including a brief time as Legislative Director for a member of Congress. So far, the last part of my career has been in philanthropy with a significant commitment to an effort I envisioned and curated called *Putting Racism on the Table*.

I tell you all that to say that as a Black woman with education and professional experience in public policy, how was it possible that I fully understood individual racism, prejudice, and bias but didn't see structural racism and didn't understand its perniciousness, depth, and impact?

Because the system, the political, social, and cultural system of our country has been built on bias and racism from its inception. It is often invisible and normalized. It's in the air we breathe and the water we drink. Everything we do is impacted by our race and our assumptions and thoughts about what that race means.

For about the last decade, I have framed my work on racial justice under the header "REVEAL, REFLECT, RECALIBRATE." Because so much of our country's racial truth has been hidden, the first step is to reveal the truth. Then, because so much of this truth will be surprising or counterintuitive for many, you must reflect on it. You have to sit back and think about the new information and start the process of learning and unlearning. To be clear, my intent is not knowledge for knowledge's sake. Yes, I want you to learn, but most importantly, I want you to act. Your action doesn't have to be grandiose. You alone cannot change racism in this country, but you can be a part of that system of change. Your action may be in your family, your neighborhood, or anywhere. I am calling on you to understand racial injustice and, when you see it, to work to change the situation.

Following the murder of Trayvon Martin in 2012, my eyes were opened to realities I simply hadn't recognized. When I shared my new insights with colleagues and friends, they often said, "I didn't know that." It was comforting and disturbing to know I wasn't alone in my ignorance and blindness.

In 2017, I created a blog to capture stories and revelations. I named it after my book: 'Daughters of the Dream' in recognition of the role my lifelong friends—the daughters of the dream—had played in helping me negotiate safely, both physically and psychologically, the racism that had always been the backdrop of our lives.

REVEALED is a compilation of fifty-two blog posts written between September 2017 and June 2023. Although some are dated, the messages remain relevant. Combined, they are a pertinent guide for your racial justice learning journey. As you read, it will be helpful for context to note when the blog was originally published.

What I know is that learning must be repetitive and reinforced. Remember how long it took to learn Spanish or perfect your tennis game. Learning about race and racism is even harder. This book offers one reading a week, just a 4-5-minute commitment.

While I think REVEALED is right for anyone beginning their racial justice learning journey, it is particularly so for the white community. Think of REVEALED as your racial justice primer. It will give white readers information and insights into an America they may not have considered. It is America, as seen through the eyes of a Black American.

I believe in the power of one, the power that each of us has to be a change agent.

It's time to get started.

Tamara Lucas Copeland, 2023

P.S. While I am not a trained historian, I have been drawn to history since I was a child. I have attempted to check and double-check all statements for accuracy. Still, I hope you will forgive any errors that may have been made.

JANUARY

I don't make New Year's resolutions. I used to, but I just found them too difficult to keep. Maybe it was the solemnity of a resolution. Can't you just hear that dark, resonant music in the background when you say the word?

What I can do is start new practices, and for some reason, I can maintain them for a long time. So, that's what I'm asking you to do. I want you to start the practice of reading and thinking about the issue of racial justice. I want you to be a lifelong learner about structural racism, bias, and our country's racial history. REVEALED is intended to jumpstart your ongoing learning with a short read once a week.

Here's the first month. I chose these posts because they set the stage for your learning. They provide some of the fundamentals for understanding race in America. I won't say anymore. Remember, all I'm asking is for you to get into the habit of reading a brief blog about racism, bias, or racial history once a week.

**"Not everything that is faced can be changed,
but nothing can be changed until it is faced."
—James Baldwin, Author**

Racial Healing

Originally Published in July 2019

America isn't ready for it.

Yet!

Over the last couple of years, I have heard a lot of talk about racial healing. I have the same reaction every time: How can we heal without treating the wound, and how can that be done effectively without understanding it?

I want America to recognize the depth of the racial wound and to acknowledge how that wound, that injury, that disease... spread and infected society.

Recently, when talking with a Black friend, she reminded me that my perspective is that of a Black person. In her view, white people want this conversation to go away. When she hears 'racial healing,' she thinks it is code for 'Black people need to get over it.' Hmmm. Get over it.

I am just beginning to understand IT; the extent and impact of racial inequity and injustice were hard for even me to see. I, too, was duped. I understood prejudice and discrimination, but I thought those who were prejudiced were ignorant people or those whose views were ill-informed because they hadn't gotten to know Black people. And then, ignorantly, for decades, I thought discrimination had ended with the passage of critical pieces of Civil Rights legislation. I believed this country was a meritocracy. I believed that if you worked hard and played by the rules, you would 'win' by American standards. I was so very wrong. I didn't understand the facts, subtleties, or biases that shaped how the world was presented to me.

It wasn't until recently that I began to fully appreciate the white lens through which many stories and 'facts' are told. Even when the recounting is not directly by a white person, the story is influenced by white culture/lore/norms. With each visit to the National Museum of African American History and Culture, or when reading posts on the blog *The Root*, for example, I get a deeper appreciation for how much I never learned of the history, the accomplishments, and the positive impact of Black people on America. And it still isn't being told in the dominant media.

It took the injustice of Trayvon Martin's murder, coupled with the lack of consequences for his murderer, to shock me out of my stupor. And it took listening to countless podcasts like *Uncivil,* absorbing the wisdom and in-depth racial analyses from leaders and thinkers like john a. powell (no capitalization is his preference), Robin DiAngelo, Richard Rothstein, Ta-Nehisi Coates, and Ibram Kendi for me to learn the insidiousness, intentionality, and impact of structural racism; the structures in place for decades causing Black people to be disadvantaged as white people moved farther and farther ahead. My learning until 2012 had been casual, family-influenced, experiential. After the horror of Trayvon, my eyes opened to an obscured reality. I started on a conscious learning journey to understand the depth, breadth, and impact of structural racism on society and me.

There have been decades of Band-Aids placed haphazardly with no real sense of where the wound was or that the injury may present as a flesh wound... a small cut, quickly addressed. But it isn't.

IT is a cancer, invasive, all-consuming. Those Band-Aids were insufficient unless their intent was not to heal but to mask the problem and the fact that no one was trying to cure it.

That's how I see the rush to racial healing. Another Band-Aid.

Even though wounds can be ugly, they must be revealed and their cause understood. That's my issue. I don't think the racial injury has been fully exposed and understood. Have people with the insights, knowledge, and sensitivity to fully determine the problem diagnosed it, i.e., has the cadre of diagnosticians gone through the educational rigor to understand the symptoms, how the problem operates, and how to treat it? Who is studying how to prevent it from returning? Who is focused beyond treatment to eradication?

Personally, I want to heal. I want America to heal. I just know that if it has taken me, a Black, educated person directly affected by structural racism and implicit bias, some time to see and begin to understand it, how long will it take those who benefit from the way the country is?

America doesn't seem ready—as a country—even to admit that racism exists, much less to learn how it occurred and how it continues. And there is no quick, easy fix. It will take years of work. Racial healing is a process, not an event. We must unspin the web that created and now perpetuates racism. Then, systematically, we must replace it with a new societal reality. Only then do I think we can heal. As the author Ralph Ellison said, "It takes a deep commitment to change and an even deeper commitment to grow."

CREDENTIALS

ORIGINALLY PUBLISHED IN NOVEMBER 2018

It may have been that Christmas when the chemistry set was more of a hit than the doll and dollhouse that Mr. and Mrs. Swann got the first inkling. Or the glowing reports coming home from the junior high chemistry teacher about their daughter Madeline. But they knew when she asked to have pet mice for some experiments. Science was Madeline's calling, and she pursued it with a purpose. In 1980, Madeline graduated from Howard University, earning a Ph.D. in chemistry.

She thought she would work on eradicating diseases but was drawn to research the properties of fuels. Working for thirty years as a U.S. Department of the Army civilian employee, they lauded her work on keeping fuels liquid in harsh, cold climates. Those testimonies to her intelligence and skill in her technical field were diminished by the number of times—in meetings and conferences—she was taken to be clerical support and asked to fetch coffee and sandwiches for the generals in the meetings who were doing the 'real' work. Once she made the offenders recognize their errors, apologies were made, and the meeting continued with Madeline playing her proper role. But Madeline's lingering feeling was that no one in those rooms—full of white men—even considered the possibility she could be the chemist on whose research their military plans were being developed. Madeline died in 2017. If she were alive today, she would have been the last person in our group to be surprised by the 2018 event on a Delta Airlines plane.

Dr. Fatima Cody Stanford, an African American physician, offered her help to a passenger having a medical emergency. Three Delta employees questioned Dr. Stanford's credentials even after she produced her medical license. This incident followed another on Delta in 2016 when Black physician Dr. Tamika Cross's credentials where questioned.

While Dr. Madeline Swann's experiences and Dr. Stanford's are decades apart, the realities are the same. Some things change, others remain. Some white people find it hard to believe Black people have professional credentials. Some suggest that America is more racially fair now than ever before. I suspect that is true. You will more likely encounter an African American Ph.D. or M.D. today than at any other time in our country's history. Still, even so, only about 6% of all physicians today are African American.

Similarly, only about 6.5% of all doctoral candidates are African American. Some might suggest that these low numbers—the low probability—underscore why Madeline wasn't considered the chemist and why Dr. Stanford was questioned about being a medical doctor. I don't believe that.

Even when presented with tangible evidence—a medical license— Dr. Stanford was not believed. Whether in the 1980s or thirty years later, the default presumption is a Black woman couldn't possibly be a physician... or a scientist. The narratives about Black people's ambition, intelligence, and capabilities are still rampant, as are other biases—some might even be unaware of—against African Americans.

In the 1990s, when another friend styled her hair in braids and put them in what she thought was an elegant and professional chignon, she was told that hairstyle jeopardized her career path in corporate America. Her hair, not her Ph.D., evidence of her knowledge and expertise, became an issue. She wasn't conforming to an American, white community-based, physical standard.

A few years ago, I heard a Black woman colleague say she had earned a Ph.D. not because she wanted to be an academic but so the white community would not question her knowledge. I wonder if that has afforded her the social and community elevation and respect, she expected.

My friends and I were raised to be daughters of the dream, a dream in which success would be possible due to the content of our character (and the credentials we earned), not limited or prohibited by the color of our skin. Today, many years after Martin Luther King's memorable address, skin color still invokes certain beliefs, assumptions, and prejudices. It is the 'credential' some see long before you can pull out your medical license or run home to get that diploma.

Equity—Not Equality—In a Post-Coronavirus America

ORIGINALLY PUBLISHED IN APRIL 2020

"It's just not fair."

You don't hear that only from your kids. It comes from adult friends and family, too. We all seem committed to a level of fairness that just isn't fair... not really.

I write my *Daughters of the Dream* blog to reveal racial truths, at least racial realities, as I see them. These "truths," like the myth of fairness, might be overlooked if not pointed out.

The situation with coronavirus offers many stark examples of these "truths" covered by a veneer of fairness. I will look at just two: health care and economic viability.

Many have said that COVID-19 shows no preference for race, gender, or income status. All—any of us—can get it. Well, that's true; by that measure, it is fair. However, we now see that susceptibility to the disease and treatment is not.

Headlines reveal that race-specific data isn't always collected. But when it is, it shows more African Americans are dying from the disease. Race-based treatment of African Americans in the health care system and more deadly outcomes isn't new. Stories from slavery reveal experimentation on enslaved people that rivals Josef Mengele in Nazi prison camps. In the 1930s, African American men in Alabama thought they were part of a research project to determine the impact of different treatments for syphilis. But their disease went untreated, and the test continued for decades. Most will know the name of Henrietta Lacks, whose cells, taken without her permission in the 1950s, form the basis of many medical breakthroughs and treatments today. But few will know the name of Sterling Matthews. A 60-year-old diabetic cancer survivor who was told in late March 2020 that he had pneumonia and was sent home by a suburban hospital in my hometown, Richmond, Virginia. He died a few days later after finally being diagnosed with coronavirus.

Our pain thresholds are perceived as higher, and the value of our lives seems to be lower. This isn't just historical. It's not in the past; it's ongoing. This is now. Is it fair? No.

The perception is the disease affects all equally, but that isn't true. African Americans are more susceptible because of the higher incidence than their white counterparts of asthma, hypertension/heart disease, and diabetes, the main conditions that the World Health Organization states place a person at the highest risk for coronavirus.

It's. Just. Not. Fair.

Stimulus checks. Everyone with an individual income of less than $75,000 received $1,200. On the surface, this appears fair, right? Everyone is getting the same amount. No money to the rich. Good. This makes sense.

If you have a regular job with the State of Virginia, for example, your paycheck has continued during this crisis. Now you are also getting $1200. Fair? What if you are a self-employed hairstylist paid based on customers coming into that now-closed shop? Or a restaurant wait-staff employee who must survive from tips no longer coming in? All making less than $75,000/year. Fair?

According to the Economic Policy Institute (EPI), a considerable racial distinction exists in who earns poverty wages. Those hourly wages would place a person below the federal poverty line if he/she were the sole wage earner for the family. 2017 data shows that African American workers are 1.5 times more likely to earn what EPI refers to as poverty wages than their white counterparts. Latinx workers are 1.8 times more likely than whites to earn poverty wages.

So, is the blanket provision of $1200 to all with incomes under $75,000 fair? No, it is equal.

It's. Just. Not. Fair.

According to many surveys of American values, equality is second only to individualism as what defines us as Americans. That needs to change. Equity, not equality, must become the new watchword for America. We must realize that we aren't all starting in the same place. One size does not—and never has—fit all.

We now have the opportunity to reshape our country in so many ways. Coronavirus has placed us on pause. What can we do in post-COVID-19 America that will help to address some of the inequities that exist?

I wish I had answers, not just insights and a few questions. I know the individualism America celebrates... that pull-yourself-up-by-your-bootstraps mentality... isn't true. Everyone who has achieved a level of success has had help. Sometimes for a single generation, but it is often multi-generational support that has bolstered a family. America must become more focused on helping those who haven't had the opportunities or couldn't avail themselves of them. The solutions are out there. Probably—hopefully—developing in the minds of those with a much higher pay grade than mine. It will take the collective thinking of economists, educators, social scientists, community organizers, and working folks to fully define the problems and barriers and then craft a new America. It can be done.

The. Time. Is. Now.

DEI MEANT NUMBERS TO ME... I WANTED MORE

ORIGINALLY PUBLISHED IN DECEMBER 2021

Recently, while co-facilitating a training on racial justice, a white participant asked a pointed question: "What is the goal?" He continued by asking if employers should mirror the percentage of specific groups of people of color in the American population or what. I could hear frustration, or maybe exasperation, in his voice. He worked for a business that had mandated its entire team go through this training. He wanted to finish the training and come away with a specific direction. A third of the way through, he didn't see the session leading in that direction, and he was right.

This was a significant aha moment for me.

That participant in the training wanted a road map. What was the quickest way for him to get from point A to point B?

Instead, I was giving him a complex route with multiple interconnected roads. On top of that, the goal was racial justice, something he may have seen as an amorphous reality, not his tangible point B.

Like many racial justice trainings, what I provided was designed to open the participants' thinking. The participants were intended to leave knowing that Black Lives Matter is more than a slogan. It is a reality, with evidence of why we haven't mattered for centuries. I want participants to understand the microaggressions and oppression Black people and other people of color face daily. The goal is for them to become allies or advocates for racial justice, with the skills to use a newly acquired lens to see, interact with, and transform the world.

That one participant wanted to know how many Black people needed to work in his business to be compliant/woke/racially just. That moment was a juxtaposition of black and white... and gray. He was in a black-and-white business world of Diversity, Equity, and Inclusion (DEI): hard numbers, measurable goals, and specific, time-driven outcomes. I was in a gray, nuanced world of understanding racial history and racial reality on the way to working for racial justice. Ongoing, forever.

I have been challenged by the concept of DEI for some time. I think of it as minimizing. This participant again elevated my discomfort while also prompting my thinking.

The term DEI—diversity, equity, and inclusion—seems to me, most often, to be translated into numbers. Those numbers are critically important. I know that. I just want so much more than numbers. A person/business/organization can do all the right things under the DEI approach and still not reckon with how race has shaped their own life or experience at work, how they may be complicit in racial injustices, or see how their company or organization perpetuates racial inequities or benefits from historical injustices.

I want participants' understanding of racial injustice to evolve through the training. I want them to be exposed to a more complete history of our country, one that, for example, discusses the injustice of not getting forty acres and a mule and how redlining and decades of prejudice and discrimination have left Black families with one-tenth the wealth of white families in America. I want participants who go through racial justice training to understand that they have been blaming the victim, consciously or unconsciously. Do most DEI programs do that?

For some reason, I heard that participant with new ears. I reflected on his question and viewpoint, realizing I needed to open my mind. I needed to align my view of an organizational or business focus on DEI with my commitment to what I perceive as a more comprehensive examination of race and racism. One is not right, and one wrong. They're different strategies, complementary, both necessary and incomplete. We need to see more racially diverse employees in every sector, at every level. And we must go beyond solely a DEI-compliant workplace to get to a racially just America.

DEI and racial justice seminars/trainings are all part of a necessary, multifaceted tool kit for social change. Various strategies, interventions, and layers of action from thousands of voices are needed to birth a racially just America. So, to my DEI-focused colleagues, I say you're doing important work; keep looking at the numbers, but also take that macro view, learn about all that has gotten us to where we are as a racially unjust country, and then go well beyond the workplace to make it right.

Don't Say That! Huh?

Originally Published in January 2022

One of the things I know for sure is that common sense or common knowledge isn't common. We each see the world through a lens shaped by family and family values, life experiences, and acquired knowledge.

I was reminded of this when a white friend commented that she'd never again say that a person's hair looked like a rat's nest, having been chastised, strongly and simultaneously, by several Black friends who heard the comment. She continued, noting that while she wouldn't repeat it, she didn't know what was wrong. She had been describing a person, not actually saying it to someone.

Without an explanation, this friend may have thought her comment was perceived simply as rude, but there was so much more.

Nuances, history, and connections would never be understood by her or other white people solely by reading books about the Black experience, racial injustice, or Black culture. That academic knowledge must be woven together. The dots must be connected to reveal why that combination of words—describing a Black person's hair as a rat's nest—evoked a visceral, negative response from the Black people in that room. Months later, Black friend-to-white friend, the following information was shared.

Rats as a sign of filth.

Neighborhood filth.

Rats are often associated with filth and dirtiness. Rat infestation indicates accumulated filth and a problem unique to some communities. The cleanliness of Black neighborhoods has often been questioned, giving many white people an "acceptable" reason not to want Black neighbors. But few know what Richard Rothstein revealed in his book, *The Color of Law*. In some cities, in the early through mid-20th century, trash was not picked up with the same frequency in Black neighborhoods as it was in white neighborhoods. It wasn't the lack of cleanliness by the residents but the racist practices of the cities that contributed to the rat problem. Is it possible that those practices continue in some places today?

Personal dirtiness.

Also built on the connection between rats and filth, a Black person would immediately think of all the myths regarding personal hygiene. The dirtiness—real in some cases, imagined in others—of Black people relates back to enslavement and their inability to have access to soap and water to bathe and, of course, the time to do so. The sentiment of Black skin as a sign of dirtiness continued in the 1800s and early 1900s, with Black children depicted as being washed with a certain brand of soap to become white. Black skin as a sign of dirtiness was seen as recently as 2017, with a Black model in a brown shirt becoming a white model in a white shirt after using Dove soap. The subliminal message is there: dirty, ignorant, lowly.

Natural hair.

Hair is a person's crowning glory. The connection between hair and your sense of beauty is inextricable. Sadly, until recently, natural hair has often been described as unkempt. It wasn't until the Black Pride/Black is Beautiful movements of the '60s and '70s that many Black people recognized the internalized racism that made them not see the beauty of their natural hair. Until then, many wanted the texture of white hair, using chemicals and applied heat to get it. But even after Blacks embraced their natural hair and natural styles like dreadlocks or braiding, many whites continued to view those styles as inappropriate for the workplace. As recently as 2019, California and New York saw the need for legislation making it unlawful to discriminate against a person based on their hairstyle or hair texture.

All this information, and probably much more, went through the minds of the Black people listening to their white friend. All of it. In the blink of an eye. They had heard a statement mired in years of subliminal racist messages. But all they said was, "Don't say that."

Months later, one of the Black people in that room, no longer able to let the comment stand, reached out to the white friend. After hearing the full explanation of why saying that a Black person's hair looked like a rat's nest was an awful comment, the white person shared that she had been describing another white person. She thought she had said that but wasn't sure in hindsight. Wow, had the Black folks assumed she was speaking about a Black person based on their life experience? Maybe an in-the-moment conversation would have been clarifying, but not speaking immediately allowed for the more thoughtful and possibly less emotional, later exploration of the topic. The white person acknowledged a bit of initial defensiveness about what was interpreted from her comment but also had three important reflections: she wants to learn more about race and culture; she appreciates those who pull her aside and educate her; and she recognizes her privilege to move in and out of discussions about race because she is not living it (hmmm ... a topic ripe for a future conversation?).

Bottom line: Friendships are built on trust. Have those conversations that need to be had; if not at the moment, have them when you can. We'll all be better off.

What Did January Reveal?

Well, how did that go? Did you read one piece a week? Okay, you forgot once, but then you read two, right? You're on your way to developing a practice. By the end of next month, it'll almost be automatic, and by the end of the third month, it will be.

Let me share why I chose those pieces to begin REVEALED. As America becomes more knowledgeable of structural racism (racism embedded in the systems and structures that shape our country), bias, and all the factors contributing to disparate treatment based on race, we're talking about it more. That's great. But I've noticed we don't seem to be using terms or concepts in the same way. I've found the glossary at www.racialequitytools.org. to be clear and useful. I urge you to check it out.

In REVEALED, I don't focus on definitions but on racial justice concepts. I've discovered that telling stories is the best way to do that. The stories in REVEALED are personal stories, or stories told to me that I've reflected on and have meaning for my racial equity learning journey. Yes, I'm still learning and understanding.

For January, I wanted to lay a foundation. I wanted to share concepts and terms often mentioned in conversations about racial justice.

Racial healing is often near the top of terms in discussions of race and racism. Many want society to heal. They believe that harm has occurred. We've processed it, talked about it, passed legislation to "fix" it, and now it's time to heal. They believe that the wound is healed. They think it doesn't hurt anymore, so let's get back to normal.

Equity and equality are frequently used interchangeably. I wanted to point out that they are very different. Remember "separate-but-equal"? The suggested intent was that Black people would get the same as white people even though that never happened. The underlying premise was sameness. However, equity acknowledges that a different

20

intervention is needed because of different circumstances to achieve the same outcome. I was trying to demonstrate that in the coronavirus intervention, I included.

I know you hear DEI often, especially in the workplace. Acknowledging the need for and benefit of a diverse community, whether at work or elsewhere, is essential. We want to embrace the importance of equitable opportunities and the need for different peoples to be fully a part of the environment, not solely there but celebrated, valued, and included. The post you read was intended to say that while important, DEI isn't enough without attention to understanding structural racism. Did that come through? What were your thoughts?

Bias has also been a hot topic. We all have it. What can we do about it? The post titled "Credentials" was about bias. We must acknowledge, work hard to recognize when it is driving our response, and then learn to do better and respond differently. Remember, the first step in repair is acknowledging the problem.

The depth of the injury and the ongoing impact was the focus of "Don't say that! Huh?" An "innocent" remark prompts a lesson in history, culture, unfair practices, and pain. Racial pain is deep and built on decades of actions. This post also intends to show that while it is important for white people to educate themselves about race, a person of color's insight is valuable in explaining the intricacies and nuances.

REVEAL, REFLECT, RECALIBRATE. With this explanation, has more been revealed? Are you ready for February, Black History Month?

REFLECT ON THESE QUESTIONS

- What was revealed to you, that was the most surprising? Why?
- Do you now understand the distinction between equity and equality? Why is understanding that distinction important?

NOTES:

FEBRUARY

I always think of love and Black history in February. The two combine in my memories of Albert V. Norrell Elementary School, my first school. Long before Black History Month was acknowledged in most schools across the country, the history was recognized, with pride and love, every day in my racially segregated elementary school, but especially during what was then called Negro History Month.

This month, I'm asking you to focus a bit deeper on Black history. To understand where we are in America, we must look at history comprehensively and truthfully, vis-a-vis the disparities between races and the Black racial reality. Sugarcoating or ignoring facts doesn't make them go away. That approach simply gives us all a false sense of how we got to where we are.

Some posts will reveal the growing emphasis that emerged several years ago on teaching Black history in schools. Sadly, that moment of commitment to teaching Black history seems to have passed in far too many parts of the country. Given the growing backlash to teaching the history of African Americans in our schools, it is even more critical that we all make a concerted, personal effort to study our country's history—fully.

> **"Until the lion tells the story,
> the hunter will always be the hero."
> —African proverb**

Missing Pieces of American History

Originally Published in May 2018

The National Museum of African American History and Culture opened on September 24, 2016. When the date was announced in February, Black History Month, I marked it on my calendar. I had already planned two trips for the late summer/early fall. Living in Washington, DC, I had been watching the building of the museum and looking for the "opening soon" signage to become a definite date. Now that I had it, both trips would have to be planned around the opening. I wasn't likely to receive an invitation to the festivities. Still, nothing would prevent me from being on the museum grounds that day. I had to be a part of this incredible event, a museum on the National Mall dedicated entirely to the history and culture of my people.

> "I was sitting at home watching the opening of the National Museum of African American History and Culture on TV. I could feel the energy, and I, too, had been anticipating the opening. I started to wonder why I wasn't there, then I told myself, well, it wasn't my museum. That's when I had the epiphany. Of course, it was my museum, mine as an American."

A white colleague told me that story a few weeks after the museum opened. I don't think he was alone in his viewpoint. Many white people supported a museum dedicated to the African American experience. Still, they weren't sure where/how/if they were a part of it. Even I thought of it as my museum and, interestingly, was, at first, surprised by the number of white people there during the first of my multiple visits.

That's the problem.

The history of Black America has never been a part of the history OF America. It always had a place, and one of significance, in Black America but little visibility in white America. My teachers and principal—all of whom were Black—in elementary school made sure I knew it. Biographies of Black Americans were prominent in the school library. Pictures and commentary on Black people and achievements lined the classroom bulletin boards and were displayed throughout the building. Not just for what was then Negro History Week but throughout the year. And the successes and milestones of Black people were the everyday conversation at my family's dinner table and readily available as both *Life Magazine* and *Ebony Magazine* were delivered to my home.

That wasn't the experience for my white colleague. No focus was placed on teaching him about Black America at any point in his formal education. Without his commitment to broadening his understanding of America, his knowledge would be driven solely by happenstance personal experiences and the manner of coverage by the ubiquitous electronic, social, and print media.

Black history had been, and still is, compartmentalized and marginalized.

In 1977, many Americans, Black and white, were riveted by the television miniseries *Roots: The Saga of an American Family*. Never had there been as mainstream and as public an examination of the history of Black people in this country. Every episode became next-day conversations at metaphorical water coolers just about everywhere. But today, four decades after recognizing how much *Roots* had revealed that we didn't know, Black history still is not fully incorporated into the American past that our sons and daughters learn in school. Black American history is still niche history, not yet seen— at least by those who control textbooks and our educational system— as a part of a comprehensive examination of our country's history.

The jigsaw puzzle of America's history continues to have too many missing pieces. But, for those who understand that gaps exist and those who want to understand the fullness, richness, and inequities born in American history, many resources exist to help with that powerful learning journey today.

History Denied

Originally Published in November 2017

Marcus Garvey, founder of the Universal Negro Improvement Association and an early advocate of Black nationalism, said: "A people without the knowledge of their past history, origin, and culture is like a tree without roots." I was an adult before I learned a significant fact about my familial roots.

I learned that my great-grandfather, Henry D. Smith, my paternal grandmother's father, had served one term in the Virginia General Assembly. But no one actually told me. By chance, after my Dad's death, I came across a booklet at his sister's home called *Negro Office Holders in Virginia, 1865-1895*, by Luther Porter Jackson. When I asked my aunt why she had it, she simply said her mother's father was in the book.

"What?" I asked in bewilderment. "Why has no one ever told me about this?"

"There was nothing to say," she responded to my astonishment and said nothing else about it even though I probed.

From the book's summary of his life, I learned he had been born into slavery in 1834. Through hard work as a farmer and distiller, according to the very brief paragraph on him, he amassed sufficient wealth to, at one time, own over 900 acres of land, including the Merry Oaks Estate, once possessed by the family that owned him as a slave. In 1879, he was elected to the Virginia House of Delegates. End of story. But that couldn't be the end. How did he accomplish this? Did he help others in the Black community with his position and wealth? I tried to get my aunt to tell me more. Finally, she did, but only a tidbit.

"Your grandmother [Mary 'Mamie' Smith Lucas] was one of his last children, born to his third and final wife, Ella Wyatt Smith, just a few years before he died in 1901."

"That's it?" I persisted.

"Yes," snapped my aunt, clearly angry. "He lost his land, cheated by the white man like we always have been. That's it." And that was all she would ever say about this chapter of my family's history.

I knew that the history of Black people had generally been denied to all of us—Black and non-Black people alike. When I was a student, it was only through supplemental education that I learned about Marcus Garvey, Langston Hughes, and Charles Drew. I imagine the white community learned even less. Nothing was taught about the history of countries in Africa, but everything about the history of England. Regardless of this larger frame of history denied, I didn't know that my family had also denied me my personal history.

As I have reflected on that, I think they may have been ashamed my ancestor was able to rise from slavery—to accomplish what anyone would be proud of—but couldn't hold on to what he had attained. His legacy was tarnished by his downfall at the hands of the white community. We were bamboozled, as filmmaker Spike Lee says. A century after his death, my aunt was still angry, and I suspect sad, about the trajectory of his life.

Wealth comes in many forms, and often, the most valuable inherited treasure is not material. It's knowing the history and stories of those who came before us. The sum and substance of the people and their stories that ultimately led to our own existence. We are poorer when it is denied us. I don't have the fullness of my great-grandfather's story. I, too, am sad that his story did not end with the glory he probably envisioned.

Nonetheless, I choose to release the familial anger and celebrate him. In the late 1800s, not a generation after the end of slavery, my great-grandfather was a landowner, a business owner, and a state legislator. My heart is full of love and pride.

Illuminating the Past and Lighting the Future

Originally Published in February 2020

The following questions were the beginning of a short quiz that was featured online as a tool for Black History Month commemorations:

Who was the first African American Major League Baseball player?

Where was Malcolm X killed?

Where was the first sit-in at a segregated lunch counter?

After each question, there were multiple choices and a place to click for more info.

Many will likely know the answer to the first question, but what if it was re-worded: "Who was the first African American allowed to play major league baseball?" You'd still know the answer, but you might think about it a bit differently. Not that there weren't African Americans with the talent, as the stated question might imply. And if you click on the "Learn more" button, you see that the argument from the team's manager isn't focused on racial justice or morality but on economics. The white owner of the team, the white manager, and the white players would all be financial beneficiaries of this change. Then, if you have time, go deeper into his story to learn about the life of this "first" and the mental anguish Jackie Robinson and his family suffered.

Then look at the second question. "Learn more" will remind you that the Black community isn't monolithic. While being Black in America offers a distinct vantage point from being white or Asian, Indigenous or Latinx, and while there may be unanimity in the desire for justice and equity among Black people, there is no shared sense of strategy. In that divergence, however, a center point may become clearer. Some suggest if there hadn't been a Malcolm X, a perceived radical, Martin Luther King's views might not have been deemed reasonable and viable. He would have been the revolutionary. That point alone could generate a vibrant discussion if you move a little beyond the presented fact.

Now to the third item in the quiz. "Learn more" reveals that in 1960, just two generations ago, Black people fought for the right to sit down and have lunch in an integrated environment. Perhaps that would have been your parents' or maybe your grandparents' generation. Where did they stand/fall on the question of Civil Rights? Have you ever asked them, or if you are the parent or the grandparent, have you ever shared with the younger members of your family what you were doing or thinking in 1960 when people were actively advocating for the Civil Rights of African Americans?

These are conversations that we should all have. Maybe Black History Month offers an entrée to this topic for your family.

Understanding a people's history isn't just about knowing the dates or being able to rattle off trivia at a cocktail party. It's about revealing and understanding the layers, actions, and reactions that contribute not just to those people but to the fabric of the bigger "U.S." as a people and as a culture. Often, those revelations and discussions happen in school. I know that is where I learned, explored, and discussed much about the country's history. My parents and community often talked about current events, but I rarely recall family discussions about historical events. And once I left the segregated school system, Black history never entered my formal education.

Over the last 50 years, Black history has increasingly been recognized as an essential part of American history... and world history, that it is. Some states now require its incorporation into the educational curriculum. Textbooks are being written. Students are asking for it. But the subject still doesn't seem mainstreamed into the curriculum. Some suggest that history and social studies teachers aren't trained to teach it. Even when they try to cover the topic, they aren't comfortable enough to delve deeply. The conversation typically stops with the facts. Others suggest many of the textbooks introduce Black history with slavery, reinforcing African Americans in a lower position in society. I'm not so sure I agree with that, even though I can appreciate the viewpoint. Black Americans' history did, in no small measure, start with being enslaved. There is just so much about that reality that can be explored. Teachers can take the lesson back to Africa.* In school, we often talked about what was happening in Europe that pre-dated white settlers coming to America. I still remember the weight of my European history textbook. Whole semesters focused on the subject, but never in the 16 years of my liberal arts education did I have one course on African history. What was happening in the countries and kingdoms there?

I don't have the answers, but I know that when Carter G. Woodson helped found the Association for the Study of Negro Life (1915), later became the chief advocate for Negro History Week (1926) and promoted the study of African American culture and history throughout his life, he was not suggesting it as an add on. He was filling a void until the topic could be fully fused into any study of the history of America.

Kasi Lemmons, the director of the film "Harriet" about Harriet Tubman, the freedom fighter and abolitionist, said, "The past should not oppress; it should illuminate." Taking a quiz or focusing on interesting factoids can start a conversation. It can begin the learning, but we must remember the facts are just where real discovery and understanding begins.

What will you do during this Black History Month? What will you do throughout the year to better understand, appreciate, and value the contributions of African Americans?

* * *

*If you are interested in learning about Africa's civilizations, check out the PBS six-hour series, *'Africa's Great Civilizations'* by Dr. Henry Louis Gates, Jr.

All I Know About Race and Racism, I Learned in_.

Originally Published in September 2020

Hmmm... I never learned this.

An article, "*Happy Slaves? The peculiar story of three Virginia textbooks*" by Rex Springston, came out several years ago. I just read it on the heels of an email from a college friend. She reminded me of what we learned in the 4th and 7th grades and then in high school about Virginia's history and enslaved people.

My 7th-grade textbook, *Virginia: History, Government, Geography*, presented enslaved people as well-treated servants, and the Confederacy was glorious with "handsome" (the language used in the fourth-grade textbook) General Robert E. Lee fighting for a noble cause. It was a fairy tale within the hard frame of history textbooks. Fake history.

As Confederate statues have come down, there have been many cries that history is being destroyed. The then-U.S. president said: "We have a heritage. We have a history, and we should learn from the history."

Well, that's the problem. The history of America, particularly its racial history, never has been taught fully and comprehensively. Many have learned a version of history through the lens of white leaders with a specific, racialized agenda, but typically not from unbiased historians committed to the truth.

When I first entered an integrated school in the 6th grade, my Mother told me: "White people don't always tell the truth." I knew she was talking about adults. Her message surprised me. I had been taught to always respect adults and thought that included expecting their truthfulness. This was the first clue that my educational experience was changing.

Every day, when I left school, I came home to a community that challenged and corrected what I had been taught in history. They shared a different story of slavery, one that revealed the atrocities of subjugation, and a different story of the Civil War, not about the battles per se, but about what was at its core. My education was augmented by information about slave uprisings and about Black people fighting for their humanity, not docile and lazy, but hard-working freedom fighters. And that history I learned from my family and neighbors was the truth.

For my white classmates, also learning from those textbooks, was the content ever questioned? I suspect there were few white households in Richmond, Virginia, in which the story of slavery was even discussed back then, much less refuted. It—the stated and printed history—just was. In the 1950s, when these textbooks were developed, Virginia led the fight against integration. The notion of Black people being happy with their current condition was mythology in 1850 and remained so in 1950. Distortion of history was taught in public schools, with textbooks developed and approved by the government-established Virginia History and Government Textbook Commission. Why would the content be questioned? It wasn't until the late '60s that a small reference to Harriet Tubman was added to appease vocal outrage from Civil Rights advocates. And it wasn't until 1972 that the Virginia Department of Education announced that the three textbooks that had then shaped thousands of students' knowledge of Virginia's history for over two decades would be "decommissioned" ... not denounced as they should have been.

So, what's the big deal now? The new history textbooks are correct, right? Maybe, but what about those who learned from the old texts? Just consider this. If you were in the 7th grade in 1972, today, you are in your 60s, perhaps still in a leadership position, probably a senior leadership position... a judge, state legislator, college professor, maybe. Think about how many people these folks have mentored over their careers. What policies have they shaped or influenced? Are these some of the folks calling for Confederate statues to remain because history is being erased? Having those books as their texts, living in racially homogeneous communities, and never learning about Black people is part of what shaped them. Philosophically, who are they? What are their values and beliefs?

And this isn't just a Virginia story. In America, we place enormous trust in our education system to prepare our children to succeed. Can you successfully negotiate America—a country developed largely by Black labor—without understanding Black history, culture, and the fundamentals of a racial hierarchy that goes back 400 years? Until now, the answer has been yes.

As an increasing number of Americans call for racial justice, there must be education. To right a wrong, you must first understand it. As noted author and thinker James Baldwin said: "I think that the past is all that makes the present coherent and further that the past will remain horrible for exactly as long as we refuse to assess it honestly." Today, there are courses and degrees in Black Studies in many colleges across the country, and some schools focus on Black history in February. However, the history of Black people and race and racism is rarely taught as a required course at any stage in a person's education, K-12, college, professional degree program, or post-graduate. It is episodic. Until this is taught as a required course or a series of classes, many white people will continue to get their history of race and racism, and Black people from the news or off-hand remarks made by their peers.

We must do better. Learning about Black history and culture, along with race and racism, cannot be ad hoc or haphazard. It must be structured, intentional, and incorporated throughout the educational experience. Moving America to racial equity will require the inclusion of an examination of racialized America in mainstream American education. REVEAL, REFLECT, RECALIBRATE. It can be done, and we should do it. Now.

What Did February Reveal?

"Black history is American history" is often heard these days. Of course, the statement is true. Take a moment to reflect on why offering such a reminder is necessary?

American history has primarily been taught as the history of white people in America, with a couple of almost parenthetical nods to the Black, Indigenous, and People of Color (BIPOC) communities. Indigenous People were acknowledged as being here when the white settlers arrived. Slavery happened, and Asian Americans built the transcontinental railroad. There was Japanese internment, Rosa Parks, MLK, and Barack Obama. Are those the historical highlights of non-white America that you remember learning?

Because of the limited nature of what was taught, the story of America has been skewed. People of color were "extras," almost extraneous. Few think, for example, about the essential role of the slave economy and then Jim Crow oppression in enabling white people to succeed and a financially strong country to emerge. You don't have an accurate picture of America without understanding Black people's contributions and unjust treatment.

Briefly, the pendulum swung toward including more Black history in schools beginning about fifty years ago. College courses on Black studies, Africana studies, and literature began to be included in many post-secondary curricula, becoming almost expected content. In the last decade, expansions of history courses, particularly on local history, had a more comprehensive examination of the role people of color played. Education was opening to a more inclusive exploration of history. Sadly, there seems to be a growing movement to delete racial history from K-12 curricula today. Proponents of this action state that they believe teaching it will harm white children and the "progress" made toward racial justice. Think about that for a minute.

So, where does that leave understanding the fullness of our country's history and current reality?

Blacks and whites don't live in close proximity routinely and fully as neighbors in many parts of the country. Racial history and Black contributions to America aren't regularly taught in school. A knowledge void remains because historical events and cultural realities aren't casually shared through neighbor-to-neighbor, friend-to-friend interactions, nor are they taught in a structured manner in America's public-school classrooms.

So, where do white people really learn about Black people? Self-education through books, podcasts, and documentaries occurs for those with interest. But, the primary source of passive education about the Black experience and reality for most is the media, which many suggest suffers the same prejudice and unconscious bias of society. Consider the following sampling of articles and studies:

- *"Report Documents Racial Bias in Coverage of Crime by Media"*—Equal Justice Initiative, 12/16/21
- *"The Pervasiveness of Racism and Bias in the Media"*—Forbes, 2/28/22
- *"A Look at Racial Bias and Inequity in Media Coverage of Criminal Defendants in the United States*—CSG Reports, 12/16/21
- *"Study Shows Racial Bias in Media Coverage of Celebrity Domestic Violence"*—Department of Sociology, University of Maryland, 6/25/23
- *"Racial bias affects media coverage of missing persons"*—NPR, 12/5/22

Multiple studies confirm the bias in media coverage, yet without structured in-school education, the media is the sole or primary source of knowledge about Black people, culture, and history for most white Americans. How does that shape the Black America that many see and believe?

REFLECT ON THESE QUESTIONS

- Is the National Museum of African American History and Culture on your list of places to visit when you come to Washington, DC? What about the Holocaust Museum? Why or why not?
- Did you learn about Black history in school? If so, what are three facts that you remember? How do those facts relate to today's reality?

NOTES:

MARCH

Every year, when I turn my calendar to March (yes, I still have a paper calendar), I immediately think of protests. March, marching, you get it? I think of marching to reveal injustices and call for change. Those grainy images from the '60s come to mind, and I still feel the calmness and fierceness of those marching for Civil Rights. Quietly and purposefully, hundreds of men, women, and children marched to protest injustices and elevate needs, always knowing that they were risking their lives.

Protest marches continue to focus attention on societal inequities on many fronts. This month's posts encourage you to recognize that we all have a role in the quest for racial justice. What is your part? What are you doing? You don't have to march to take action for racial justice, but you do have to act.

> **"One has a moral responsibility
> to disobey unjust laws."
> —Dr. Martin Luther King, Jr.**

White People, Step It Up

Originally Published on May 7, 2020, before the May 25th murder of George Floyd.

Picture this. The coronavirus is over. Scientists have given the "all clear." One million white people have gathered on the Mall in Washington, DC, with signs that read "Black Lives Matter," "I am marching for Ahmaud Arbery," "I march for Trayvon Martin," "I march for the thousands of Black men and women imprisoned who simply can't pay bail to get out" "I march for clean water in Flint" "I march for quality grocery stores in Black and brown neighborhoods." "I march for the Black people who white leaders don't listen to."

Can you see it? Can you see one million white people marching for Black lives, for Black bodies?

I appreciate all my white friends who have posted their outrage on social media about the killing of Ahmaud Arbery. I value your allyship and your sense of humanity. I also value your public statements. Many think the thoughts but then don't write the words where one of their friends, family, or colleagues might see them. "You know," they say, "I have to pick the right moment."

White people, as Nikole Hannah-Jones wrote in her *1619* essay, "Our democracy's founding ideals were false when they were written. Black Americans have fought to make them true." I'm not saying that white people didn't participate in the Montgomery Bus Boycott, Selma, the March on Washington, or countless other protests to make America's promise come true. You have. But I need you to step it up. America needs you to step it up.

Now, don't get me wrong. Black people's voices have been, and continue to be, powerful in enabling our liberation 400 years ago, 200 years ago, and today. But to paraphrase racial justice advocate Dr. Robin DiAngelo, "Could women have gotten the vote without the leadership of men? No." Black people can march and will march until the soles of our feet are raw. We will protest until our voices are strained to a whisper, but white people, we need you to step it up.

In considerable measure, your people run Congress... your people lead states... your people run business, the Fortune 500 companies... your people control the media. You run America. Raise your voices. Step it up.

Are You Working for Racial Justice? How?

ORIGINALLY PUBLISHED IN MARCH 2022

I'd like you to reflect on a racially just America.

What would it look like? What would you see—in your neighborhood, on the news, at your workplace, in your child's school? Think about the steps/strategies/tactics necessary to get there. Now, sit back. Relax. Reflect on these questions for a few minutes. Is an action plan forming in your mind, or are you already engaged in this work?

Some folks have told me they work for racial justice by volunteering at a local foodbank (or another social service agency) or tutoring disadvantaged children. I used to cringe silently when I heard that. Not anymore. Now, comments like those are conversation starters.

America has a rich and necessary history of volunteerism. During economic downturns and times of human need, donations to foodbanks, for example, and volunteers to hand out food are critical. These actions keep people alive. When we look at food lines, we often see people of color disproportionately represented depending on the location. While donating and assisting at the many agencies helping people in need is important, this is not racial justice work—even if those sites primarily serve Black and brown people.

The work is essential. It is lifesaving. It is humane. It simply doesn't work for racial justice. It doesn't change, or help to change, the racial imbalance.

Racial justice work would prompt you to consider: why do Black and brown people predominate among the needy in many communities? What are the conditions and circumstances that create this level of disproportionate need? What am I doing to change those conditions and circumstances?

Thinking about those questions might still lead you to see your work as a tutor as racial justice work. Tutoring –> better grades –> college –> good career opportunities –> a level playing field. If only we lived in a meritocracy in which this trajectory was real, but studies have proven that this is not the case for many, if not most, Black and brown people in America, and those differential outcomes start early in a child's life.

So why do some people see strategies like those as working for racial justice? Just because the beneficiaries are Black or brown, is that it? It certainly feels good to volunteer. But, in some situations, I also see a negative side. Volunteering in social service or education programs clearly positions the haves and the have-nots. While it may not be at the forefront of thinking, subconsciously, could there be some feeling of superiority? If the children are underprivileged, are you overprivileged? You have the financial resources. They don't. You have academic credentials. They don't. How does volunteering at the foodbank address the employment conditions contributing to food insecurity? Does tutoring change educational systems or hiring practices? I know the response: It helped that family. It helped that child. Yes. Just don't call it work for racial justice.

In racial justice work, there are allies and advocates, partners, and collaborators, but there are no haves and have-nots. Everyone is equal, bringing their perspectives and strengths to the table. This is the model of mutual aid societies in which all members bring something supporting the needs of others. Each gives, and each receives. Assets, not deficits, are the driver. Mutual aid, not charity.

So, I offer two resources for those truly interested in racial justice work. Corrine Shutack's article listing 75 ways white people can support racial justice went viral in 24 hours and continues to grow as new ideas are added. It and Ibram Kendi's *How to Be An Antiracist* are two of the best guides. But you don't need those resources, not really. Look around you—your neighborhood, your child's school, workplace. If you deeply reflect on what contributes to racial injustice in some aspects of your world, you'll see your role in changing that. The accumulation of multiple actions by many people leads to the societal change necessary to achieve a racially just America.

Again, my intent is not to diminish or devalue volunteering at social service organizations or working to improve educational outcomes for children. I simply want to underscore what actually contributes to racial justice.

As Dr. Martin Luther King, Jr said, "Philanthropy is commendable, but it must not cause the philanthropist to overlook the circumstances of economic injustice which make philanthropy necessary." The service of the volunteer—their "philanthropy"—is often a stop-gap, albeit valued and valuable, measure to solve an immediate, individual need, not an effort toward correcting a societal wrong. Those working for racial justice look beyond the immediate need to examine why those needs exist in larger numbers among Black and brown people and then work to change those circumstances. That's racial justice.

Popcorn and Picketing

Originally Published in January 2018

"Are the picketers out today?" a voice on the telephone asked, already knowing the answer. When the expected "Yes" response came, the caller replied, "Okay, then we won't be coming to the movies today. They make the lines too long."

At the time, my Dad was the manager of one of the Lichtman movie theaters, a chain of segregated theaters in Washington, DC, and across Virginia. Movies were a significant form of entertainment in my childhood. So, it wasn't unusual for a group of us to munch on popcorn and hot dogs and drink cokes during a Saturday matinee at the Booker T, named for Booker T. Washington, or the Walker, named for Black entrepreneur Maggie L. Walker. We didn't know they got the movies a little later than the white theaters, only about ten blocks farther down Broad Street. And because we couldn't go inside those movie houses, we didn't know of their interiors' opulence. Many of the whites-only theaters truly were old Hollywood movie palaces. Perhaps the most distinguished in Richmond was the Loews Theater that opened in 1928. The Loews was called that day.

The voice on the phone was that of Debby Anderson Smith, one of my forever friends, one of the daughters of the dream. Debby was only in junior high school when she made those calls. Remarkably, at the young age of 12, she had figured out a meaningful way to be a part of the Civil Rights movement. She was the youngest of three children. Her sister, Anna, was in college, and her brother, Bucky, was in high school in the early '60s when the Civil Rights movement reached Richmond, Virginia, our hometown.

Perhaps because she had older siblings, Debby, unlike the rest of us, had a deeper understanding of the movement. While we were sheltered from the conversations about protests, she heard them. She watched as Anna, a student at historically Black Virginia Union University, left home with her sandwich board to picket the downtown department stores. Thalhimers and Miller and Rhoads, like all the major stores of the time, denied Blacks access to the upstairs fine dining rooms. She watched as her dad and Bucky drove to Washington, DC, in August 1963 to participate in the March on Washington. And she watched as her parents regularly drove neighbors to the picket sites. Debby wanted to do something like her sister and brother, but her mother thought she was too young and that it was too dangerous.

That's when Debby came up with her plan. She understood a fundamental part of the protest strategy: denying revenue to businesses got the attention of the power brokers. The protesters didn't just march. They stood in line with others to purchase a movie ticket even though they knew they would be denied; therefore, the lines were long—very long—to get into the theater. When protesters were there, other customers wouldn't want to stand in those long lines, so the theaters lost money.

Simple calls telling the theaters that someone chose not to spend their money with them because they were being protested against was also Debby's way of having her voice heard. This was how she supported the movement.

While in hindsight, we all felt we had played a role in the Civil Rights movement simply by getting an education, dressing a certain way, talking a certain way, and being primed to walk through the doors of opportunity when they opened. Little did we know, until recently, that our friend Debby played an active role. You go, girl.

A Picture is Worth a Thousand Words

ORIGINALLY PUBLISHED IN AUGUST 2020

Many people characterize Washingtonians as living in a bubble. Maybe. But if we do, there is diversity in that bubble. I live in a section of Washington, DC—Capitol Hill, Ward 6—45% African American and 42% white. Walking through my neighborhood, I see people who look like me. Older African American women are among the early morning walkers, exercising around the park near my home. Some people appear to be Asian American or Latinx. There are people speaking languages I recognize, and many I don't. Young people push baby strollers, and folks, young and old, on scooters and bikes and dining in outdoor restaurants. The diversity of my neighborhood is one of the many things I like about it.

Capitol Hill has become whiter over the years since I've lived here. Gentrification is a term used regularly when discussing my part of DC. Still, lately, I've noticed Black and brown young couples choosing to move into this community, not just white families.

Regularly in the *Capitol Hill Corner*, an online neighborhood newsletter, you learn of new shops, restaurants, condo buildings, and grocery stores coming to the Hill. And this week, I learned of a new women's clothing store moving into my neighborhood. That's great, I thought and was excited until I clicked on the link to their website.

So glaringly unexpected it took my breath away. I had to look twice. There were 22 images on the opening page (yes, I went back and counted). Shocking in its whiteness, there was not one Black or brown model. The models all presented as young, slim, and white. Judging by this store's marketing message—conveyed by their images—I was definitely not their desired customer. Wow. I felt excluded. I was excluded.

I get it. This store is marketing to young women. As I reflected on it, I realized it wasn't the lack of age range in the models or the lack of varied body types I found disturbing. It was the lack of racial diversity. While clothing stores and advertisers across the country recognize diversity in size, shape, age, and race, this store has stepped back in time. It seems entirely out of step with what I hope to see in my neighborhood.

So, I contacted the store with my concern. The owner responded in less than 24 hours. She noted that she was an immigrant and wrote: "I deeply value inclusivity and take pride in our mission and commitment to diversity—it's the heart and core of our company." She then referred me to the company's Facebook and Instagram accounts. Both sites had more diversity—nominally. But I stand by my initial reaction. What the owner says she values is not reflected in the primary image projected by the company, the home page of its website.

No, this store's marketing is not a big deal in the fight for racial equity, but the look and feel of your neighborhood is developed: one business, one school, one grocery store, and one family at a time. We are all responsible for taking steps, large and small, to build the racially just and welcoming community we want to live in. Just a reminder: when you see something, say something.

* * *

P.S. I don't believe that public shaming is the most effective first strategy to affect change. For that reason, I chose not to mention the store's name in this post. I hope my note will open the eyes of the boutique owner, leading to new thinking and actions. I'll let you know.

P.P.S. A 2023 look at the store's website revealed different races and body types. Good.

WHAT WILL YOU RISK TO FIGHT RACISM?

ORIGINALLY PUBLISHED IN OCTOBER 2022

I just finished reading *Crusade for Justice: The Autobiography of Ida B. Wells.* I suspect many are unfamiliar with her name and her work. This African American journalist, born into slavery in 1862 in Mississippi, was among the first to speak out against lynchings. Loudly and continuously, she used her voice to say that lynchings were not the legal punishment for falsely stated rape or disrespect of white women, as was often suggested. Sexual assault was the deceit. The real crime, committed consciously or simply by accident, had disrupted the established racial norm. A Black person had overstepped. At a time when Black people were persecuted and killed for any number of actions, but particularly for questioning or acting against established racial practices, Ida B. Wells spoke up. She did not allow any threat to her safety to silence her response to injustice. She was fierce.

Throughout history, many have risked their lives for what they knew was right... fair... just.

Others have stood by, seeing injustice, and said and done nothing— afraid of the risks.

Which camp do you fall into?

What will you risk for racial justice? Friendships? Community standing? Financial benefits?

Will you:

51

- Speak up when a friend, family member, neighbor, or acquaintance makes a racist comment?
- Speak up when coverage of a news event seems to be biased against one race or group?
- Speak up when a policy proposed by an organization with which you are affiliated or employed seems racially unfair?
- Decline work that contributes to racial injustice?
- Recommend interventions to promote racial justice in spaces where you have a voice?
- Promote learning (books, podcasts, documentaries) and actions that will broaden the knowledge of people in your sphere of influence about race, racism, and reparative justice?

Can you say yes to all of the above? If not, you are more afraid of what you might lose than what you might gain. Instead of a commitment to racial justice, you are worried that a person won't still be your friend if you speak up about a comment they made or an action they took or that your neighbors will shun you if you say something about racism at a community meeting, or that you might risk advancement or maybe even your job if you speak up. Those are real concerns. Just know that if you have them and if they stop you from speaking up, regardless of your heartfelt sentiments, you are enabling racism.

When former quarterback Colin Kaepernick decided to kneel during the national anthem to showcase the inhumane treatment of Black people by police, he risked his career and lost it. But he elevated an issue and demonstrated integrity. More recently, while not working for racial justice, Congresswoman Liz Cheney spoke up against a different type of injustice—treason. She knew she risked her position in Congress, but she did it anyway. Like Kaepernick, she gained the respect of many and demonstrated integrity and a moral consciousness even while losing her position.

Your profile may not be as public as that of Colin Kaepernick or Liz Cheney, but the loss is relative. Yours might be as significant as losing friends, community stature, or even a job. Only you can decide what you are willing to risk and possibly lose.

We must take racial injustice as a personal affront. We must learn that some things and people aren't worth holding on to if they jeopardize society. Think about it. Reflect on it and decide if you are genuinely an antiracist, ready, willing, and able to take a stand for a better society, a racially just America. I hope so.

What Did March Reveal?

When you are made aware of or see racial injustice, racially biased behavior, or individual racism, what is your response?

Regardless of where you sit in the world, you have the ability—and I think, the responsibility—to act against racism, to be an antiracist. Often, people believe racism is too big a problem for one person to make a difference, but we can all make a difference. You don't have to be the person addressing the biases recently revealed in value appraisals of homes, for example, or the person repairing the structural racism that lurks in our educational system. You can be the person who notices that the white person wasn't asked for identification when using a check to pay for a purchase, but the Black person was. You can say something. Or you can be the person who notices the dearth of architects of color at the architectural firm you're about to hire and ask why. Or you can speak up when your neighbor/friend/uncle makes a racially derogatory comment. It's not okay. You can act.

The challenge is two-fold: 1) knowing what to say and how to say it, and 2) accepting the risk of taking a stand.

This month, there's an extra reading assignment. Go online to the Southern Poverty Law Center. Look for *Speak Up: Responding to Every Bigotry*. Here are a few chapter titles: What can I do about joking in-laws? What can I do about boss bias? What can I do about biased customer service? What can I do about stubborn relatives? This is an easy-to-read primer that will guide you. But you have to plan ahead so you're ready when the situation arises. Take the time to read this resource so you are literally primed for the offender. This isn't the only resource, but it's free, accessible, and a great starting place. No one wants to be chastised publicly. Consider the words to use and where to share your observations and concerns. Ultimately, you are trying to increase understanding and change behavior. This will take time, repetition, and explanations, but with care, you can make a difference.

Then, you need courage. When you speak up against racism, you make a choice that may position you differently, perhaps in direct opposition, to someone you love, have respected, or admired. You are taking a risk. Think about those who marched in the 1960s with big dogs snarling at them and powerful water hoses pushing them down. Or think about those who walked into schools as their fellow students spat on them and yelled obscenities. Think about watching George Floyd be murdered in May 2020. Think about the world you want for your children, the opportunities, the safety, and the pursuit of happiness. All that the Declaration of Independence decrees for your children and grandchildren, I want for mine, as do all other Americans. Your voice And your actions can make a difference. Massive change starts with one disrupter, one pebble that ripples out. You can be that agent of change.

REFLECT ON THESE QUESTIONS

- Had you ever heard of Ida B. Wells?
- What was the last action you took to fight racial injustice? Think about it. Was your act really fighting racial injustice, or was it a Band-Aid or a stop-gap measure?

NOTES:

APRIL

April brings optimism. Spring represents rebirth. So much is possible. This month's posts focus on shifts/growths in thinking and shifts in understanding race and racism.

I told you that my first moment of true racial clarity was the murder of Trayvon Martin and the lack of punishment for his murderer. Those events put racial reality into a very different perspective for me. Certainly, I had known prejudice and injustice. And I had had glimpses of racial understanding, but Trayvon was my ground zero. As my racial equity lens strengthened, I started seeing the world differently, asking questions, clarifying, reading, and asking more questions. I began to see the extent of bias and structural racism.

When did that happen for you? What was your first aha moment about the distinctions between Black and white reality in America? When did you really see how much race matters in America? What gives you hope that we can achieve racial justice?

"I am no longer accepting the things I cannot change. I am changing the things I cannot accept."
—Angela Davis, Academic, Activist, Scholar, and Self-described Revolutionary

Awakening Racial Pride, Racial Understanding

Originally Published in April 2018

For each of us, there is an awakening. Something that has been tolerated is simply no longer acceptable. Sometimes, it is a moment when the reality is suddenly crystal clear. Sometimes, it is more of a process over time. For me, and for many of my high school classmates, it was a process of racial understanding and emerging racial pride that began one fall day.

> "I wish I was in the land of cotton,
> Old times there are not forgotten,
> Look away, look away, look away, Dixie Land."

Played by the school band, that's what we heard freshman year when we walked into the gym for our first pep rally. Students sang loudly and enthusiastically as they stomped on the wooden bleachers. The energy in the room was palpable.

"Dixie" was the fight song for my high school, John Marshall, in Richmond, Virginia. Yes, that "Dixie." The song born in the minstrel shows of the mid-1800s, the song that was the standard for Confederate soldiers during the Civil War, and the song that had come to represent the collective of the Southern states and the Southern sensibility in the United States. That "Dixie."

This was the mid-1960s. Brown v. Board of Education had called for integrating all public schools about a decade earlier. Still, schools in Virginia were slow to recognize the mandate. In fact, they actively worked against it. John Marshall was still a predominately white school with few black students when I arrived. Many in the all-white school administration and among the white students' parents had fought against integration. Black people were actively trying to prove that they could fit in. Like most at the time, the Black students at John Marshall were Negroes, integrationists, and assimilationists. No one wanted to do anything to cause trouble. Black people were trying to gain acceptance in a white world. And on that fall day, the white and Black students were just kids cheering their football team as the players entered the gym.

We were all children of the cultural South. We all knew the words. By rote, almost everyone sang with little regard for the meaning or essence of the song,

> "In Dixie Land, I'll take my stand,
> To live and die in Dixie."

A traditional fight song for the South, a song of pride, it had probably been the rallying song for John Marshall High when the school opened in 1909, just a little over 50 years after the Civil War. No consideration had been given then to any culture other than white, and little was offered over fifty years later for Black students. It is unlikely that anyone—not for a moment—thought this, a school rallying cry, might be offensive. Did it really matter?

Something about singing the song probably felt wrong from the start, but we went along to get along. Then, one day, the words suddenly came into focus. Our consciousness had been raised. The school rallying song did matter. It was symbolic of so much. How could "We Shall Overcome" be the song of the times—more importantly, the anthem of our people—while we continued to sing "Dixie?"

Students asked the administration to stop playing "Dixie." They were disregarded. Then, one day, in our junior year, the Black band members—in one catalytic moment—decided to take action. They didn't refuse to play the song; it could have been played without them. Their effort was far more effective, demonstrating the song's effect on us— it was hurtful. When the band director called for "Dixie," the Black band members played other songs, not just one song, but many. Cacophony resulted, then silence. That moment of dissonance accomplished what polite requests had failed to do. In that silence, was there any racial understanding or compassion? I don't know, but "Dixie" was no longer the fight song for John Marshall High School.

WHAT MAKES ME HOPEFUL

ORIGINALLY PUBLISHED IN APRIL 2022

When I learn more about the history of Black and brown people in America or am confronted by the latest racist act or inaction, I realize I am often in a space with just two emotions—anger and sadness. Anger and sadness that my people have faced such hardships and inhumanity. Anger that racism still thrives in America. Sadness that so few seem to embrace the will to achieve racial justice. When I realize I have these feelings, I think about what gives me hope and then repeat a powerful quote from South African political activist and president Nelson Mandela, "May your choices reflect your hopes, not your fears."

I am hopeful when I go to my hometown, Richmond, Virginia, and interact with young activists committed to challenging the system, utilizing new tactics, and continuing the fight for racial justice.

I am hopeful when I read a friend's Facebook post about her white yoga instructor in Vallejo, California, who closed her class asking for prayers for the people of Ukraine and continued by offering prayers for the Black and brown people in Ukraine who were forced to let white people leave first.

I am hopeful when a blog reader tells me she is white and 80 years old and asks me not to give up on her demographic's role in understanding and working for racial justice.

I am hopeful when a white friend in Florida notices that the Google pictures for a nearby majority Black community feature only negative imagery of Black people and then does something to change that.

I am hopeful when an all-white group of college friends decides to pursue a deep examination of some of the racial elements of our school—William and Mary—its community—Williamsburg, Virginia—and our country's current racial reality.

I am hopeful when a foundation board on which I serve commits fully to learning, understanding, and investing in pursuing racial justice through its support of Black and brown-led organizations and -owned businesses.

I am hopeful when the Richmond Public School system embraces a supplemental curriculum called REAL Richmond, focused on the parts of Richmond, Virginia's racial history that aren't in the textbook.

When thinking of what makes a person hopeful about the pursuit of racial justice, some might point to the president's selection of a Black woman as his nominee for the Supreme Court or the multiple efforts across the country to protect voting rights for people of color or Evanston, Illinois, an evolving case study in how a municipality can offer reparations to the descendants of enslaved people. These are interventions that will have a deep, meaningful, long-lasting impact. They represent significant change, change writ large.

At the same time, I recognized that each action started with one person finally getting it. One person who understood racial injustice and acted. And that one person may not have known what an inspiration they were to others. Often, seemingly small, isolated steps lead to institutional and societal change that will ultimately ensure racial justice.

What are you doing that gives hope to others? Five years from now, who will recognize you as the inspiration that sparked their work for racial justice?

When Did Black Become Beautiful for Me?

ORIGINALLY PUBLISHED IN DECEMBER 2017

The definition of beauty is elusive, subjective, and changes throughout one's life. In fact, the concept of beauty, witnessing it or thinking someone is beautiful, is really an adult term used with adult sensibilities.

'Cute' was how we wanted to be described in high school, and my friend Jeanne Johnson was cute. Everyone thought so. She was bouncy and vibrant, always with a big smile and just the right, witty comment to perk up any conversation. A member of our then club, the Valianettes, she is now one of my forever friends, another daughter of the dream. In 1968, she was crowned homecoming queen at John Marshall High School, the first Black homecoming queen at a predominantly white school in Richmond.

We couldn't contain ourselves as we cheered and jumped up and down in the bleachers. A Black homecoming queen was something we had wanted since our sophomore year. In our junior year, with some degree of political astuteness, we had orchestrated a bloc voting campaign to make it happen. We focused on the one Black candidate, hoping the white kids would spread their votes over their five nominees, but they championed just one candidate, too.

In 1968, things were different. Jeanne was announced as THE homecoming queen at the year's biggest football game. And it wasn't just the Black kids cheering for Jeanne. No bloc voting this time. No strategy. She had simply won. The white kids cheered, too.

Jeanne was popular school-wide, but it wasn't just popularity being acknowledged that fall night. It was also a beauty contest. This was still the era in which girls and women were judged most heavily on their appearance. Back then, beauty was defined by white criteria: fair skin, long, straight hair, and curves but not too plump were the day's standards. There had been no Black Miss America yet. No Black girls were on the cover of *Seventeen Magazine*, nor did we see many who looked like us on television.

That year, Jeanne was recognized as THE girl, the all-around girl—smart, popular, and pretty—to represent the school. Her selection as homecoming queen was a breakthrough. But it would still be many years before dark, brown-skinned girls were acknowledged for their beauty or natural hair was seen as the magnificent crowning glory we recognize today. And the plus-sized beauties that seem plentiful in the Black community are, even now, just beginning to get their due. Mocha-skinned, wavy-haired, curvy-in-the-right-places, Jeanne was a visual bridge between what had been and what was to be.

Not only has our societal standard of beauty changed to be far more inclusive, but so have the rules we use to define women. Just a few years after Jeanne was named Miss Justice, Helen Reddy released the song that would become the anthem of the women's movement. Its powerful first line, "I am woman hear me roar in numbers too great to ignore and I know too much to go back and pretend," encapsulates how women were beginning to see themselves: strong, capable, aware of the past, and positioned for the future.

Given that Black women had been working for as long as anyone could remember, many saw the women's movement as the white women's movement. Perhaps. But no one can deny that doors opened for Black women, too. Jeanne and all of the Valianettes are a product of the civil and women's rights movements. Jeanne, becoming homecoming queen, foretold so much more to come.

Can New Friendships Grow 50 Years Later?

Originally Published in November 2019

I have a lot of friends. Some are closer than others. I think I understand what it takes to build and maintain a friendship: shared experiences over time, mutual respect, and similar values.

In the Fall of 2019, I attended a milestone high school reunion. John Marshall High School, Richmond, Virginia, Class of 1969. I suspect that for many, a 50th reunion is a long-awaited event to renew acquaintances and recapture friendships. It seemed to me that a lower percentage of Black than white graduates attended. I wonder if both groups did not share fond memories of high school equally.

The '60s were a time of significant racial change in Richmond and nationwide. My high school started the decade as a primarily white institution and finished as a mostly Black one. White flight was real. The John Marshall class of 1969 was probably the last one with a white majority. Our class felt the impact of the changing demographics. I attended the 40th reunion. Then, the Black and white students, including me, mostly stayed in our old high school cliques, with only nominal mingling at the reunion.

The prospect of the 50th reunion felt different. As an inveterate traveler, I even passed up a trip to Greece with another group of friends to attend. I guess it may have been more important to me than I wanted to admit.

I entered the first event of the reunion weekend with a bit of trepidation. "Cautiously curious" would best describe my emotions at the Friday evening Meet-and-Greet. There was a much different feeling from the 40th reunion. This time, the mood was welcoming and inclusive; people seemed genuinely happy to see each other. Racially mixed groups—genuine laughter and what-seemed-to-be real conversations—were what I saw and experienced. That feeling of camaraderie continued at the weekend's culminating event, the dinner dance on Saturday night.

What happened between 2009, our 40th reunion, and 2019?

A significant conversation about race had started in the United States. Did that play a role? Did we understand the dynamics of race in a way we never had before, and did that understanding make basic conversation easier?

Over the decade between the 40th and 50th reunion, cell phone videos captured startling displays of injustice that could not be ignored. Newspaper articles, magazines, and television documentaries layered messages about racial inequity throughout the popular media. And great attention to the topic surrounded the presidency of our country's first African American president. Awareness of race and the disparity between races had probably become more prevalent in America during this decade than since the Civil Rights movement when our connections as classmates were forming. Maybe these discussions and events were a factor in making the encounters across race more genuine. I wonder if the heightened understanding made it easier to walk up to people of a different race and start conversations. We did, after all, have a shared framework—the halls of John Marshall—if not a wholly shared experience. Maybe that recognition of only recently revealed parallel universes opened some conversations.

When speaking at the dinner, Carolyn Mosby, one of the few African American faculty at John Marshall when we attended, said to the group, "Tonight we will throw back any regrets, any dislikes, any old grudges." In those words, she recognized that many Black students had felt prejudice, discrimination, aloofness, and racism during our time at John Marshall High School. She acknowledged that some white students, consciously or unconsciously, may have hurt their Black fellow students through words or actions. That was real, but she wanted us to move on. Ever the teacher, she was helping us bridge any existing racial chasms and recognize the passage of time.

Regardless of race, we had all been young with the callousness and insensitivity of teenagers. AND we were the front guard. The mid-to-late '60s were still the early days of integration. When we were in high school, there was not even a semblance of a road map for understanding racial differences and promoting honest dialogue across races. There were no experienced guides. We plotted that territory. Mrs. Mosby reminded us to cut each other some slack. We were all very different now than we had been fifty years earlier.

That is an important reminder. We must give each other room to grow, change beliefs, and adapt to new understandings of historical "facts" and current reality. Who we were does not reflect who we have become.

I don't have white friends from high school, at least not yet. In the last few years, I have crossed paths with a growing number and enjoyed those connections. We are friendly, but not yet friends. But who knows, some budding relationships may evolve into real friendships by the next reunion.

What Did April Reveal?

When I look at some of the statistics for our country and some of the policies being promoted, it is easy to feel hopeless.

- According to the Federal Reserve, in 2022, white households had assets totaling $124.5 trillion. Black households had assets totaling $8 trillion. This is not a typo!
- According to the U.S. Bureau of Justice Statistics, Blacks comprise 12% of the population and 33% of those imprisoned. Whites make up 63% of the U.S. population and 30% of the imprisoned. What contributes to this disparate reality?
- According to the National Center for Education Statistics, 40% of Black college students graduate from a 4-year college within six years compared to 64% of white students. How does this reality impact possibilities?

The list of disparate outcomes by race could go on, but from just these three facts, you can see why I sometimes alternate between being angry and sad. From the very beginning, there has been an uphill struggle, always fighting against what, at the time, seemed like insurmountable odds.

That's when I remember. There have been abolitionists and allies, freedom fighters, and warriors for justice since America's earliest days. Some of the names we know, but others are those unsung heroes who served as stops on the Underground Railroad, the nameless young people who were Freedom Riders, those who marched in 1963, and those who marched in 2020. They are my high school classmates who knew that "Dixie" shouldn't be the rallying cry for our school and that beauty came in all skin colors and hair textures. They are the young lawyers in the Innocence Project or the thousands mentoring young people to keep their eyes on the prize and support them when obstacles get in their way.

Today, I am hopeful when I see the progress made in representation in many aspects of America—state legislatures, Congress, NASA, park rangers, and oceanographers. When I look in toy stores and children's store bookshelves, I see a rainbow of skin tones and facial features that reflect the whole of humankind, not just one segment. Black people have succeeded, jumping over hurdle after hurdle. I know this and all the new obstacles that quickly rise with each success.

The posts selected for April were intended to give us all the hope we need to continue fighting racial injustice. We can't overlook the racial reality reflected in the statistics above, nor can we casually dismiss those opposed to teaching the true history of our country, for example. But those are the facts and the people who energize us. They give us the fuel we need to keep fighting. Years ago, racial justice activist Rev. Jesse Jackson coined "Keep hope alive." Those three words energize me. What gives you hope and keeps you moving toward racial justice?

REFLECT ON THESE QUESTIONS

- When did you realize that many Black people had a different perception of America than many white people? Why is that understanding important?
- Do you have a close friend of a different race or ethnicity? For you, what characterizes a close friendship?

NOTES:

MAY

It's fully springtime. Maybe you're like me, and walking is one of your favorite things. As we move toward Memorial Day, and you walk around your community, look around. Who is your city celebrating in statues? Who does your county or town memorialize?

There's been a lot of reflection and action recently, particularly around statues of Confederate soldiers and places named for them. Some say take down the statues of those who defamed and attacked our country. Others say to leave them but give them context. It's interesting to note that there are no statues of Nazis in Germany, but here there are hundreds of statues and memorials across the United States to the Confederacy or those who fought for the Confederacy.

While looking at who is celebrated in your community, think about who isn't. Are there statues or memorials for people of color? Are any Civil Rights heroes commemorated in your community in statues or monuments? Is the institution of slavery acknowledged in the statuary? This month's posts urge you to reflect on who we celebrate and memorialize, who we don't, and why.

"The statues were symbols. Symbols matter. We use them in telling the stories of our past and who we are, and we chose them carefully. Once I learned the real history of these statues, I knew there was only one path forward, and that meant making straight what was crooked, making right what was wrong. It starts with telling the truth about the past."

—Mitch Landrieu, former mayor of New Orleans

IN THE SHADOW OF STATUES: A WHITE SOUTHERNER CONFRONTS HISTORY

Confederate Statues and the Day of Reckoning

Originally Published in June 2020

In June 2020, the statue of Jefferson Davis, the president of the Confederacy, was toppled. It had stood on Monument Avenue in Richmond, Virginia, since 1890. Virginia's governor had already announced he would remove the 60-foot-tall statue of Robert E. Lee, the figurative centerpiece of this avenue dedicated to Confederate leaders. But as evidenced by the messages written on that statue over the spring of 2020, the governor's announcement was too little, too late for those protesting the brutal murder of George Floyd and championing what was beginning to be fully understood: Black Lives Matter.

Any child of the South, as I am, knows the statues weren't only to celebrate the leadership of the Confederacy. The statues were to celebrate white supremacy. Most of these icons were erected between the late 1800s and the early 1900s. They were intended to underscore that the South may have lost the war, but in other ways, they had won. The sentiments of the South—the true belief of most white leaders across America at the time—was that white supremacist leadership would not be threatened by the mere act of ending slavery. That message was delivered powerfully through legislation and actions—Jim Crow laws, lynchings, and the prominence of the Ku Klux Klan—along with the construction of these massive statues.

Now, roughly a century after that period, citizens call for a reckoning. The Jim Crow laws, lynchings, and prominence of white supremacy have been largely camouflaged in modern times, as

Michelle Alexander revealed in her book, *The New Jim Crow: Mass Incarceration in the Age of Colorblindness*. Policies and practices to maintain the predominance of white rule, white privilege, and white supremacy have been prettied up, as my Dad used to say. Look carefully, though, and you can see where and how institutions and systems routinely give white people advantages over Black people.

But you don't have to search widely for symbols of the Confederacy. Confederate statues are abundant. Confederate flags are flown proudly across the country, even included in the Mississippi state flag. The image is displayed on bumper stickers and incorporated into clothing. The statues and Confederate memorabilia were—are—intended as a reminder of the underpinnings of the Old South and that the South— at least its philosophy on race—could rise again. But today, in many quarters, even that iconography is beginning to be relegated to the past.

In 1945, after World War II, the Allies banned all symbols of the Nazi regime. Flags were destroyed. Statues were taken down. Displaying the swastika was declared a crime. Nazis deemed criminals were sought, arrested, and tried at Nuremberg. Everything that celebrated Hitler and his thinking disappeared from Germany. There was clarity. The philosophy of white Aryan superiority might continue to live in the psyches of some Germans. But no public venues would be created to celebrate what the government saw as the most shameful time in its nation's history.

When an end to apartheid came to South Africa, there were trials— truth and reconciliation. The oppressed and the oppressor were brought together to acknowledge the pain and try to move the country to heal.

In the (re)United States, not only were there no real punishments* for the South after the war, but the sentiments of the South also seemed to shape the post-war values of the entire country.

The government of America has never addressed the racial core of the Civil War. That's the crux of the issue: America has never come to terms with slavery as this country's original sin, nor has it recognized the ongoing subjugation of Black people.

Maybe until now.

Today, we, the people, proclaim it is time for that day of reckoning. The tearing down of these statues is a beginning, moving the country from the symbolic dismantling of the Confederacy to substance: an examination and recalibration of all the elements of America: health care, education, housing laws and practices, banking and business, the judicial system, and so much more. All that underpins how America operates and ensures the advantaging of one race over another must change.

The dictionary says that the day of reckoning is "when one is called on to account for one's actions, to pay one's debts, or to fulfill one's promises or obligations." That sounds right to me.

* * *

*Note: The forty acres promised to formerly enslaved people to start their new lives was to come from 400,000 acres confiscated from Southern landowners by the federal government. That would have constituted a punishment, maybe even the beginning of reparations, but that land was ultimately returned to the original owners.

P.S. – The Mississippi state flag was changed in 2020, removing the image of the flag of the Confederacy.

Should the Robert E. Lee Statue Remain?

Originally Published in August 2020

I live in Washington, DC, but Richmond is my home. I don't get there often, but I was there in the summer of 2020 and drove down Monument Avenue for the first time since the removal of the statues of Confederate icons and soldiers. It was a sultry Sunday afternoon in July. Summertime in Richmond. Few cars. Few people.

I stopped at the pedestal that once held the statue of Jefferson Davis, president of the Confederacy. It surprised me. I felt nothing. When a Richmond friend texted me early in July that the Stonewall Jackson statue was coming down—now, right then—I immediately started surfing the channels. For hours, I streamed reports from a Richmond TV station, watching transfixed as something I couldn't imagine ever happening... happened. So, when I stopped at that pedestal, I expected to feel some emotion—joy, relief, happiness— something. But I stood in front of it and felt nothing.

I drove on to the statue of Robert E. Lee. It was always the centerpiece that loomed over Monument Avenue. And there it was. Still standing, but oh so different. Instead of the cold solemnity and haughty arrogance I remembered, there was a vibrancy, an energy I could feel even before I got out of my car. There were a few vendors at a respectful distance, and some people walked around the monument with reverence for what had become a memorial for lives lost to police brutality. I felt the power of the entire tableau.

The Robert E. Lee statue was still there but no longer proud and majestic. The dignity of that plaza now rested solely in the messages written vibrantly and boldly across the pedestal—a rainbow of reds, blues, yellows, and greens. Before my eyes could read any words, my spirit took in the colors so alive, blending from one into another. Then, as I focused, the first word that registered was "TAMIR" in huge block letters, honoring 12-year-old Tamir Rice. Slowly, I circled the statue. Some messages were profane—F_ _ _ the police—but most were profound, with BLM or Black Lives Matter appearing multiple times as I rounded the pedestal.

History is written upon that statue now—a far more complete record than ever offered before. Huey Newton's name is there. Marcus David Peters* is memorialized there, along with George Floyd, Breonna Taylor, Philando Castille, and many more. The words "2nd place" appear several times, possibly noting that this general was not the winner of that war. There's also: "No justice, no peace." When I look back on pictures of this statue from just a few weeks before, I see the messages have multiplied. The anger—bottled up for decades, centuries—has spilled out in many of the words and phrases and organic thoughts reflecting what the community feels must be said: "Black Transwomen," and "Whose schools?" and "Whose streets?" Statements, more than questions.

Yes, Robert E. Lee is still there, but what made his society then and what made ours in 2020 was clearer. Written in bursts of words and names and painted with a stark explosion of colors.

Lee doesn't only represent the Confederacy. He represents white supremacy, not just a hundred and fifty years ago but in the predominance of white leaders in statehouses, media, and businesses today. He represents a narrative seeded, nurtured, and blossomed in America for 400 years. And this is not just about individuals who shout hateful words and wave the flag of those defeated in a long-ago war. It is about a culture and a way of life that has only recently started to become acknowledged: a way of life that advantages white people and disadvantages Black people and other people of color.

I am glad that the effigies of the Confederacy on Monument Avenue are being removed. Maybe that is why I was surprised by the profundity of seeing Lee at Marcus David Peters/BLM Plaza. Raw and confrontational. Keeping the statue there—with its modern-day messages—provokes different thinking. It juxtaposes a white historical marker against today's racial reality. Maybe we learn more by seeing what's been changed but is still there—that collocation of past and present—than simply the vacancy of something that had been.

Context is important. Just a thought.

* * *

*Marcus David Peters, a teacher, was a 24-year-old Black man killed by the police in Richmond in May 2018. Peters, thought to have had a mental health crisis, was unarmed and nude when police tasered, then shot, and killed him as he continued to approach them. The police were cleared of any wrongdoing.

What's in a Name? A Lot!

Originally Published in August 2018

In September 2018, Barack Obama Elementary School in Richmond, Virginia, opened its doors for the first time.

Well, not really. The school, originally named J.E.B. Stuart Elementary, opened in 1922.

I walked to J.E.B. Stuart on the first day of the sixth grade. I had attended the segregated Albert V. Norrell Elementary School for the 1st through the 5th grade (the highest grade at that school). Even though Stuart had grades 1-6, and my 6th-grade year was well after the 1954 Brown v. Board of Education desegregation decision, for me, the 6th grade was the first year that the city fathers of Richmond, Virginia, allowed me into a white school.

Norrell and Stuart were within easy walking distance of my home, but Stuart was closer. I lived two blocks south of Brookland Park Boulevard. Stuart was two blocks north. Brookland Park Boulevard was the dividing line separating Black Richmond from white Richmond. The neighborhoods on both sides looked the same—the same beautiful mature trees, the same mixture of architectural styles of houses—but we knew it was not the same when we crossed the boulevard. While the street was rather ordinary, it represented a significant cultural divide. We were foreigners entering the all-white community where our school was located.

As an 11-year-old, I didn't think anything about who J.E.B. Stuart (a Civil War general for the Confederate states) was, just as I hadn't thought a lot about the eponym of my former school, Albert V. Norrell (an African American educator whose granddaughter, Faithe, was one of my first-grade classmates). The names of the schools were just, well, the names of the schools.

In recent years, as the racial consciousness of Americans has grown, how the Civil War is reflected in our day-to-day lives has become an important and somewhat contentious topic.

There is no question that for over a century, through many mechanisms, heroic status was given to the leaders of the Confederacy. Literally, looking at the plethora of enormous statues memorializing them across America, and especially in my hometown, gives these men a mythic place in our country's cultural narrative. And when that fact is coupled with the reality of few monuments or memorials that acknowledge the suffering of enslaved Africans or celebrate Black Americans' many contributions, you can see why the existence of the statues and the relevance of names is questioned.

Based on input from the community and students, J.E.B. Stuart Elementary School's name was changed to Barack Obama Elementary. Good, right? Hmmm.... I certainly don't want to celebrate J.E.B. Stuart, and I never did. I wish to honor President Obama, but it feels strange that now I will tell folks that I attended Obama Elementary. Why is it strange? Because he would have been a one-year-old when I attended that school. Weird, right?

As I considered that, my first thought was that long-established schools wanting to change their names should select non-current historical figures or something meaningful to the community. J.E.B. Stuart Elementary could have become Azalea Elementary, maybe recognizing the beautiful spring shrubbery in the Richmond area. Or even Northside Elementary after the section of town where the school is located, or perhaps be named for another historical figure like Albert V. Norrell, the name of the now-closed Black elementary school. Following that practice would mean you wouldn't end up with this peculiar time-warp feeling that challenges me just a little now.

What something is named does matter, having an unconscious effect on some but a significant impact on others. This year, 96.4% of the children attending this school will be children of color, with 91.8% African American. I know that the parents who hold their hands as they walk into Barack Obama Elementary on September 4th will feel a sense of pride. That pride will flow into the children as they learn about the leader for whom their school is named. And on those rare occasions when called on to mention my elementary school experience, the new name will catch on my tongue, at least at first, but I, too, am proud to have attended the only school in Richmond, Virginia, named for the first African American president. Time-warp be damned.

Another Statue Comes Down, Celebrating Protest Art

Originally Published in April 2023

Walking in my neighborhood a few years ago, I saw a tiny art installation. The sculpture was called "Stepping into His Shoes" and featured President Obama rising into Abraham Lincoln's shoes. I loved it. What a great use of a 19th-century fixture—a fire department call box—for a 21st-century message. Again, my neighborhood came through with quirkiness and public art.

Then, months later, I saw something disturbing. Obama was gone, forcibly removed from the art installation. I immediately thought, "Why do people deface art?" That thought was followed by a meaningful memory. I recalled my reaction to what I called embellishments to—not defacement of—the pedestal of the Robert E. Lee statue in my hometown.

That statue unveiled in 1890, towered on its pristine white marble base over Richmond's Monument Avenue for over a century. When George Floyd was murdered, I was supportive as graffiti grew on the pedestal in response. For me, the addition of those thoughts not only contextualized the statue but also took away any power it may once have held.

So, when the public art removal/change/embellishment aligns with my worldview, it's okay, but when it doesn't, it's defacement. Wow. I need to think about this.

The Lee statue was offensive because it celebrated the leadership of someone who chose to denigrate and subjugate my people.

I celebrated the Obama-Lincoln statue because it recognized the leadership of someone I admired. I suspect that Obama was removed by someone who felt as much distaste for Obama as I felt for Lee.

Now what? Who becomes the arbiter of public art? What is built? What stays? What goes?

The same people as always. Those in power.

My understanding is that public art, art paid for with tax dollars, is typically approved by a panel of reviewers chosen by an appointed or, perhaps, elected official. Some group supposed to represent the community's sensibilities makes the decision.

In the late 1800s, in Richmond, the former capital of the Confederacy, there was significant support for the erection of the Lee statue. His nephew was then Virginia's governor, and many wanted to celebrate Lee, the South, and Southern sentiments. It is reported that 100,000 people attended the unveiling of this 60-foot-tall statue.

I guess the lesson here is to ensure that the people in power in your community share your values. Those values will be reflected in big issues, like how they vote on policies with profound and long-lasting impact, and in somewhat lesser decisions, like who is celebrated in public art.

And, when your values are not shared by those in power, it's vital to remember your power—the power to vote out those officeholders and the ability to organize a public outcry against what doesn't align with your values and those of others in your community. That's what happened in Richmond. The Lee statue was removed amid significant public support, nationally and locally, for racial justice in public policy and public art.

Now, here's the kicker. Unlike what I thought, "Stepping into His Shoes" is not public art, at least not as I described public art above.

A little research revealed that while some call box art in DC was approved by the DC Commission for the Arts and Humanities, a public agency, that wasn't the case with the art piece in my neighborhood. No public dollars were used to create it, nor was public input sought. No? No, but it's located on a public street—East Capitol—in a structure owned by the District—the vintage call box. Does that make it a form of public art? I now know that "Stepping into His Shoes" is another example of protest art, not public art, as I had thought. When I saw the Obama-Lincoln statue, I only recognized their coupling as philosophical kindred. The art said much more, but I didn't initially see that. I was again reminded of the wisdom of author James Baldwin. He said, "The purpose of art is to lay bare the questions that have been concealed by the answers."

So, when a protester removed Obama from the small art installation, I noticed. That person's act caused me to look more closely. Not just kindred spirits, the statue had also been an artistic plea by a group called Fearless Girls 2020 to replace "Emancipation," a figure of Lincoln located a few blocks away with a statue of Obama.

Did the removal of Obama deface the art, enrich it, or both? You decide.

What Did May Reveal?

Memorial Day is probably what you think of as your calendar turns to May. Planning that family gathering may be top of mind, but, like most Americans, you know that Memorial Day isn't just another occasion for a family picnic; it is the day for Americans to honor veterans who died defending the country.

What most don't know is the roots of the holiday. It was in Charleston, South Carolina, where freed Blacks and white missionaries decided to honor the Union soldiers who died in the last year of the Civil War while being held by the Confederacy. In May 2020, *Time Magazine* reported that they did this by decorating the soldiers' graves. Three thousand Black schoolchildren marched around the area, and Black ministers delivered speeches. According to Pulitzer Prize-winning historian David Blight, in his 2001 book *Race and Reunion: The Civil War in American Memory*, this May 1, 1865, recognition of the Union war dead in Charleston—Decoration Day as it was called—was the genesis of Memorial Day. Black history.

Twenty-five years after this event, a massive statue of Confederate General Robert E. Lee was unveiled in Richmond, Virginia, with 10,000 welcoming the statue to the city and between 100-150,000 attending the May 29, 1890, dedication. In the years following the Civil War and through the Jim Crow era, almost 2,000 structural commemorations were built to honor the Confederacy. While some suggest that these memorials were simply to recognize historical events, others believe the statues were intended to intimidate Black people and be a constant reminder of what was and what could be again.

The May posts acknowledge erecting statues and naming monuments, schools, military bases, counties, and streets for Confederate soldiers, individuals who fought against, not for, the United States. For over 100 years, the ubiquitousness of these names and statues and their impact on the Black community had either been celebrated or ignored. It took the televised murder of George Floyd to open the eyes of many to racially based harm in many aspects of American culture, including Confederate statues.

Open your eyes to what is celebrated in your community. Now it's time for that family gathering.

REFLECT ON THESE QUESTIONS

- Do you know much/anything about the racial history of your city or town?
- Who – specifically who – is celebrated publicly with monuments or named buildings in your community? What did the person do to merit that honor?

NOTES:

JUNE

Weddings, graduations, backyard barbecues. Who are you inviting to the special occasions in your life or just the everyday gatherings of neighbors and friends?

While our professional workplaces might be diverse, our friendship groups are often far less so, and our neighborhoods would often pass the definition of being segregated. How does this segregation affect how you see people who don't look like you? What are the stories you tell yourself about people with whom you don't have a close relationship? Why do you live where you do? When was the last time a person of color was a guest in your home? Why or why not?

I don't believe that white people can understand the Black experience without having close personal relationships with Black people. We need friends who will say, "Don't say that," like the post in January, friends with whom you can express your lack of knowledge and desire to learn. Without that, your knowledge is superficial and may even be an inaccurate interpretation of reality.

This month's posts will prompt you to consider your relationships with people who don't look like you.

"The most profound message of racial segregation may be that the absence of people of color from our lives is no real loss. Not one person who loved me, guided me, or taught me ever conveyed that segregation deprived me of anything of value."
—Robin DiAngelo

WHITE FRAGILITY: WHY IT'S SO HARD FOR WHITE PEOPLE TO TALK ABOUT RACISM

Intentional Conversations Among Friends

Originally Published in November 2021

It was my first trip following COVID vaccinations. I went to the Outer Banks in North Carolina with friends I've known for almost 20 years. We met through a local leadership program, Leadership Greater Washington. And over several years of restaurant dinners, happy hours, traveling together domestically and internationally, and staying in each other's homes, we've bonded. We are friends.

On the Outer Banks trip, only six of the nine of us could travel. For the first time, I focused on our racial composition: Cuban American (1), Black Asian American (1), Caucasian (4), and African American (3). And that led me to think about how this diverse friendship group discusses—or doesn't—issues of race.

That we are real friends is essential to this conversation. Two decades ago, my neighbor, Jim Myers, who is white, wrote *Afraid of the Dark: What Whites and Blacks Need to Know About Each Other.* In his book, Jim commented on the rarity of genuine friendships between people of different races. Postulating that if you don't spend time in someone's home, you really aren't friends. I think he's right. I have many colleagues and associates with whom I have casual connections, but my true friends are those with whom I spend quality time. We play together, eat together, vacation together, and talk about our personal challenges.

Often, friendships go back to our early years or to college. We developed personal connections on the playground, through scouting programs, in church, or in the college dorm. Or they develop through friendships with the parents of your children's classmates or at work. All those connections are driven by proximity—where you live, work, or play. And, where we live seems to be critically important.

That's part of the challenge for cross-racial friendships; we don't live in the same community.

According to a report released last year by the Brookings Institution, even though our country is more racially diverse than ever, our neighborhoods are not. How can we become friends who have deep, meaningful, sometimes uncomfortable discussions about the impact of Confederate statues in the main square of a small town or the importance of having a comprehensive—factual—examination of our country's history, for example? Where will those conversations happen? How will they start?

My Leadership Greater Washington (LGW) group doesn't live in the same neighborhood. In fact, we live all over the tri-state area of the District of Columbia, Maryland, and Virginia. None of us worked together when we originally convened. We often comment that we may never have met each other without LGW and its firm commitment to developing deep and lasting connections. And even within this group, the small group of nine, race-related conversations rarely happen. Why is that?

Even for friends, there seem to be boundaries we don't cross. We've been told, directly or indirectly, that discussing issues of race in racially mixed groups is taboo. Everyone is afraid to say the wrong thing. Everyone is uncomfortable. Race and racial discord aren't a happy, carefree topic that promotes laughter and camaraderie at that neighborhood cookout or office outing.

So, here's my question: How do we elevate racial issues, learn different perspectives, challenge thinking, and arrive at heightened understanding if we don't even talk about race with our friends?

I can think of several times on the Outer Banks when my LGW group might have had a rich conversation about an issue with a racial element. We all would have learned something from the conversation, and I know we could/would have done it respectfully and earnestly. Here's my lesson: We have to seize the moment when it occurs. The teachable moment.

I'm committing to making these conversations happen (or at least trying to make them happen). Not every time, but occasionally, truthfully, and fully. If we all did that, we might make more substantial progress toward a racially just America. So, let's talk... really talk. And listen.

Is Racial Injustice Becoming Clearer?

ORIGINALLY PUBLISHED IN FEBRUARY 2021

Police activity around the January 6, 2021, Capitol insurrection and the 2020 marches for racial reckoning looked very different. In less than 24 hours, mainstream media was comparing those responses. Peaceful protesters vs. armed insurrectionists. BLM vs. MAGA.

The image that aired most often showed National Guard troops stationed in the summer of 2020 on the Lincoln Memorial's steps, protecting the monument, compared to a complete lack of the same to defend members of Congress as people climbed the walls of the Capitol in January 2021.

While January 6th sickened and angered me, I had two positive thoughts:

For the first time in recent history, at least that I can remember, no Black person was killed or severely injured to focus white America's attention on disparate racial treatment. No George Floyd, Ahmaud Arbery, Breonna Taylor, Jacob Blake....

Black people didn't have to point out that there was a different police response to a primarily white crowd than to a largely BIPOC one. That difference was widely and almost immediately noticed, becoming a vital and consistent part of the story.

Does this mean that racism is becoming less invisible? I think so, and that's good.

But it is not the entire story.

Racism—personal racism and structural racism—is becoming more visible. I'm just not sure that's true for most of America. Consider these three categories of folks:

The large segment of our country that denies racism (remember Ambassador and former SC Governor Nikki Haley on the first night of the Republican National Convention: "America is not racist," she extolled as she claimed her immigrant status and Indian heritage). These folks believe anyone can succeed in America if they follow the rules and work hard. No need to look deeper. Racism is not the problem. Work harder.

The group that thinks they understand racism and disparity. They want to help, but they often focus on the surface, on prejudice and bigotry, not on the vast, hidden iceberg of injustice below.

The truly segregated white Americans rarely think about Black and brown people. Out of sight, out of mind. Not on their radar at all unless prompted by a media story (media stories that often contribute to fear of the "other").

It's the last category I want to focus on a bit.

Many white Americans live, work, and play in segregated parts of America. Not just rural America, as you may think, or suburban America, but all of America. They have limited contact with people who don't look like them and rarely think about it. Racial segregation is their norm. Others proudly claim they live in a racially diverse community or city. Still, you discover that's not so when you probe a little. They live in a racially homogeneous enclave within that city, in the next county over, or even 20 miles away from the part of the city—typically the inner city—allowing them to claim racial diversity, in name but not in reality.

I mention this because we are far more likely to understand people different from ourselves when we live, work, and play with them. Not just one environment (usually work), but all of them. Live and Work and Play. When different people come to your home, work with you, and regularly enjoy leisure activities with you and your family, those are your friends. Those are the people you care about. Those are the people you want—really want—to achieve the American dream. It is those folks you seek to understand, and it is for those people that you will see what prevents them from achieving their goals.

Don't get me wrong. I'm not saying you have to be best buddies to understand the humanity of people who don't look like you or to work for racial justice. Clearly, that is not the case. The racist behavior of individuals or racially unjust actions of groups seem clearer to many now and is regularly called out. White allies are seeking truth and working actively for societal change. However, for many, something must prompt you to understand a people or a topic far afield from your everyday existence.

Yes, the invisibility is diminishing. I was glad for the two positive signs last month. But racial ignorance remains powerful in many corners of America. Until we address that, I fear racial justice will remain far away.

WILL WE EVER REALLY LIVE AS NEIGHBORS?

ORIGINALLY PUBLISHED IN MARCH 2023

Recently, I drove through my childhood neighborhood, Northside, in Richmond, Virginia. It was a pretty, spring-like afternoon. Battery Park, the neighborhood park two blocks from my house, was full of activity. All the tennis courts were being used, and kids were playing on the basketball courts.* I saw adults, old and young, walking or sitting on their porches enjoying the day.

It is as lovely a neighborhood today as I remember growing up there over 50 years ago or visiting my Dad twenty years ago. There was just one different thing. Everyone I saw was white. Everyone. My neighborhood had been Black.

Gentrification? Not exactly.

This neighborhood didn't decline, and then wealthier people moved in. Surprisingly, this little enclave stayed pretty much middle-class for decades. People kept up their property, the lawns were tended to, and there was never trash on the sidewalks or streets. This neighborhood simply moved from a stable, white community in the 1920s, '30s, and '40s to a Black, middle-class neighborhood in the '50s and well into the early 2000s when white families started to trickle back in. Now, it's a white neighborhood. Why?

Why aren't young Black families moving into this community?

The homes seem desirable to me. The neighborhood is walkable. The park is an asset. What is missing?

I asked a Richmonder for an opinion. Here's the gist of that response.

When buying a home, Black families may make more permanent housing decisions than their white counterparts. They can't move into a neighborhood where the schools aren't good because they may be unable to afford private schools. They need to know that the amenities in the area will grow, not falter, and close. Unlike their white counterparts, Black young people may not have family resources to fall back on should their housing decision in the city not work out. Black families are more likely to purchase a forever home. White families may see it as a starter house. And while Northside has generally withstood that test of time as far as maintenance of the housing stock, it still doesn't have those cultural markers of a stable, middle-class, white neighborhood—a Starbucks or a Whole Foods. The community is seen by some as risky. Seemingly, white families can take the risk. Black families can't.

Hmmm... this theory makes sense to me. Once again, the racial wealth gap is a critical factor.

As I reflected on that, I had another shock when I went out to dinner in Churchill, a historically Black section of Richmond. Churchill was the area in which my Mother was born and raised. For most of my young life, Churchill had been an all-Black community. In the '60s, my grandmother was forced to move when a transit improvement—the building of a bridge—wiped out her immediate neighborhood. Even with that, Black folks stayed in the community. In the late 1970s, white families drifted back into this neighborhood. At that time, it was just a few people here and there. Last weekend, as I drove through historic Churchill and dined in a Churchill restaurant, just like in Northside, I only saw white people.

I was reminded of a phrase that James Baldwin made popular: "Urban renewal means Negro removal." The transit decision that affected my maternal grandmother's home was mirrored in my paternal grandparents' reality. The building of a new highway in the '50s decimated their all-Black neighborhood of Jackson Ward. The financial and social status of the Churchill and Jackson Ward residents made them of little concern to the powerbrokers in Richmond. Just as the wealth gap is a factor today in housing decisions, it was decades ago when my grandparents were impacted by racism.

I reminded myself that I am fortunate. Unlike my parents' experience, my childhood house is still there, and the neighborhood is very much the same even though the residents have changed. I was sad not to see young Black families enjoying the area as I had. I began to wonder if we will ever see really integrated communities. Not ones with a few of that kind of person, or this kind, but neighborhoods that don't tip to one race or ethnicity, one religion, or one sexual orientation, which seems to be the pattern. I'm talking about a residential equilibrium where all are welcome like those yard signs say. Is that even possible?

* * *

*The Battery Park amenities—the tennis and basketball courts—were left from when the community was all white.

Out of Sight, Out of Mind

Originally Published in June 2022

Concern often ebbs when a problem isn't constantly before you, directly impacting you. Sadly, it seems to happen regardless of the seriousness of the issue or your degree of previous commitment to address it. This is especially true when you don't understand how you are impacted by the problem, which seems to be someone else's problem on the surface. That's the situation as I see it with racial justice. Top of mind—always—for Black people. Out of sight, out of mind... often... typically? For white people.

It looks like 2022 became the year racial justice fell off the social justice map. The May 2020 televised murder of George Floyd galvanized the country. Finally, many white Americans understood why the slogan, Black Lives Matter, had emerged as a rallying cry, and they joined in the push for racial justice. For a minute, it seemed that Black lives did matter. It appeared that white people understood how racist narratives had shaped, or misshaped, their perception of the truth of America. They were digging deeply into a topic that many had only scratched the surface of before. Now, interest in learning about race and racism seems to have waned, as have many public efforts to fight for racial justice. Not only are states banning the accurate teaching of our country's history, but books on our racial history and our current reality that once dominated the *New York Times* nonfiction bestseller list are no longer there. Staff training on racial equity has slowed as businesses, governments, and nonprofits seem to feel like they've checked that box, or other social justice concerns have popcorned to the top. Is it my imagination? Has the multi-racial moment/movement ignited by the murder of George Floyd come to an end without fanfare and much notice?

Black people live with the trauma and reality of racial inequity and injustice daily, never needing any reminders beyond day-to-day life. Many white people seem to need "punched in the gut," horrific, visual moments to be jolted into racial awareness. Moments like Mamie Till Mobley's raw despair as she grieved over her son Emmett's battered body, the national coverage of water hoses and snarling dogs attacking peaceful Civil Rights protesters in Alabama, or the plethora of cellphone videos of racially-charged incidents in a hotel lobby, a college dorm, a park, or just about anywhere. These incidents sparked momentary outrage and commitments to racial redress. The images, in 1955, 1963, the 2010s, or 2020, got many off their sofas and into the streets to protest or the voting booths to elect individuals committed to change. But the commitment and passion in white communities seem to be rarely sustained. I want to know how to change that.

Understanding and addressing racial injustice is not a one-and-done situation, not reading one book, participating in one racial equity training... or voting once for the "right" candidate. There must be lifelong learning and unlearning of years of messages and then working, in many ways, big and small, for racial justice. I thought the heinousness of George Floyd's murder and many high-visibility, recorded racial incidents might be enough, but it doesn't seem to be. While race and racial justice remain top of mind for Black people all the time, for white advocates, other issues seem to have pushed race and racial equity to the back of the proverbial bus.

Racial injustice cannot be recognized and understood only by Black people. White people must see this, too, if we are to have a racially just America. White people must believe that justice for Black people will also enable justice for them. White people hold the reins of power in America. Just as women wouldn't have gotten the vote without the commitment of men, Black people alone cannot overhaul all the policies, procedures, and practices that undergird racial inequity in America. Black people can identify issues/inequities. Black people can march, protest, and vote. Black people can define and humanize the impact. Still, Black people do not sit sufficiently in those positions that wield the power necessary to transform racist systems and institutions.

White people, you must engage on this topic, not just in the moment of a hate crime like the recent ones in California and Buffalo, but on an ongoing basis. Black people must not die to prove that America continues to be racially unjust. Black people must not die to prompt white people to act. How do we sustain the commitment of the white community to work for racial justice? I really want to know. I need to know.

Swimming in Inequity: Waters Divide

Originally Published in July 2018

What do you think when someone says, "Let's go to the pool." A fun place to meet friends, a peaceful spot to read a good book, take a refreshing swim, or do laps?

Whatever you think, this iconic image of summer rarely brings forth thoughts of race, but that's precisely what happened to me recently. The racial overtone of swimming pools came to mind when I learned of a play called #poolparty coming to my area. Based on an incident that happened years ago in Mt. Rainier, Maryland, a community just outside of Washington, DC, this play focused on the unique and perhaps unexpected role that swimming pools played in the history of race in America.

Public pools were off-limits for many African Americans during the years when I grew up. In the late 1950s and 60s, there were none available for Black people in Richmond, Virginia. City leaders claimed that tight budgets and the fear of transmitting diseases, particularly polio at that time, were the basis for this decision. But no one believed that. The real reason, some suggest, was a desire not to mix races in what many felt was the intimacy of a swimming pool. Body-revealing bathing suits and the possibility of touching, even accidentally, brought forth the white community's historical need to protect white women from Black men. Since integration in civic areas was now legally mandated, public pools, at least those in Richmond and in many other communities, would be closed.

Now, this reality didn't have too much impact on many whites. There were private community pools and private country clubs. White teenagers still had pool parties, and white parents took their young ones to pools to learn to swim.

That wasn't the case in my community. Even though neither of my parents could swim, they both wanted me to learn. I remember them talking about how much fun I could have. Right before school ended in the 7th grade, these conversations started in my home. Swimming had never come up before. I didn't know there hadn't been a place for me to learn to swim until then. The local Black Y—separate and unequal— didn't have a pool like the white Y. At the time, there was no country club for the Black community. But that summer, a resource became available. A local Black physician opened his nearby home to swim instructors from the Black Y. They held classes in his backyard pool. That year, the summer between the 7th and 8th grades, I packed my towel, put on shorts over my swimsuit, and walked the few blocks to Dr. Jackson's house to learn to swim. Just as had always been the case, the Black community found a way to care for its own. But for those not fortunate enough to have a Dr. Jackson with a pool in the neighborhood, their grandparents might not have learned to swim. Their mom and dad might not have been encouraged to learn if they didn't. And the fun and value of learning to swim may not have been transmitted to the current generation.

The lack of access to pools in the '50s and '60s continues to impact today.

Swimming is often seen as a recreational activity, but learning to swim can save your life. Even today, the USA Swimming Foundation estimates that 70% of African Americans cannot swim. Consider that fact against the high percentage of people who died in New Orleans due to Hurricane Katrina, a devastating Category 5 hurricane in 2005. Most were poor and Black... and they drowned.

While access to swimming pools is still disproportionately more available in white communities, swimming and access to a pool is not the preeminent symbol of racial inequity in America. But the next time you sit by the pool to read or invite your friends over for a swim, at least acknowledge that this, too, represents the racial divide that continues to exist and is emblematic of a much more profound and significant racial disparity in America.

What Did June Reveal?

You're halfway through the year and your new racial equity learning practice. It is a practice by now, right? You've read a lot and reflected on that reading. What are the top five points that stand out for you so far?

Is recognition of the invisibility of racism in your top five? I hope so. I hope you have discerned how you must probe to discover how a policy, practice, or program might advantage one group over another. You must actively look below the surface, forcing yourself to ask critical questions as you use your sharpening sense of racial justice.

If you are Black or brown, have there been any new insights? I often tell people, as a Black person, I have always understood prejudice, discrimination, and individual racist behavior, but I had to study and focus to see the full impact of racial bias and to understand how deeply embedded racism is in the systems that form our country.

If you are white, has reading about America from a Black perspective and from a person with a racial justice lens provided you with new insights? A white person can go through their entire life without having meaningful conversations about racism and without being forced to understand racism—its depth, breadth, and impact on all of us. Do you see that now?

It's almost July, and you are midway through an educational effort that hopefully has opened you to learning more. Are you subscribing to podcasts or watching documentaries you wouldn't have noticed in your TV guide, or have you added books on racial justice or history to your reading stack? I hope you have.

I also hope you have a learning partner of a different race than your own. I know that many say that it's not the responsibility of Black people or other people of color to educate white people about race and racism. I get it. For some, it is exhausting and traumatizing, but not for all. While reading, watching, and listening is valuable, I don't minimize the value—and, in my opinion, the necessity—of conversations, particularly cross-racial discussions. Having the opportunity to speak candidly with a friend, to ask why some comment is offensive, or action is inappropriate, is part of the learning process. While we can be empathetic and open, we can't walk in someone else's shoes. We don't have the decades or centuries of culture that have embedded something in our souls. Certainly, we are all a part of the human race. Still, that minuscule part of all of us that divides us into our unique racial or ethnic groups makes a difference that impacts our lives in significant ways. Having a guide/translator/interpreter accelerates and deepens the learning process.

Only with intentionality is the depth of bias and racism revealed, and it is only with intentionality that recalibration—change—occurs. No one group can foster that change. We must work together for understanding and change.

REFLECT ON THESE QUESTIONS

- What race or ethnicity predominates in your neighborhood? Why do you live there? Do you think the racial makeup of the community was a factor for you in choosing it? Why?
- Did you know that once integration was federal law, many public places, like swimming pools, closed instead of integrating? Consider the depth and meaning of that action.

NOTES:

JULY

Independence Day and summer vacations are often top of mind. This is the time to think about the founding fathers and their victorious fight for freedom. Patriotically, picnic tables are often covered with red, white, and blue tablecloths as family and friends gather for the festivities.

Rarely do most think about the almost 100,000 enslaved people who, at the time, lived in what was to become the United States. The opening words of the Declaration of Independence, "We hold these truths to be self-evident, all men are created equal," defined a false framework for the country from its inception.

As you celebrate the 4th of July this year, think about the posts you are about to read. Who was independent? Who enjoyed those freedoms that were fought for in 1776? How did the creation of a country rooted in humans being unequal transition over time to the country we live in today?

**"This Fourth July is yours, not mine.
You may rejoice; I must mourn."
—Frederick Douglass's speech
"What to the slave is the Fourth of July?"
delivered on July 5, 1852, in Rochester, New York.**

Does the American Flag Represent Red, White, and You?

Originally Published in October 2020

A few years ago, my neighborhood was trying to define a communal look. Some neighbors already flew the American flag and suggested the flag as our shared identifier, the hallmark of creating visual cohesion. Several other neighbors almost screamed their objection to the American flag, noting that it did not reflect their values.

I was recently reminded of the angst of that neighborhood conversation. First, on the anniversary of September 11, I remembered our country's collective patriotism back then against a shared enemy whom we couldn't even identify. Flags flew from car antennae and front porch flag posts, and many were teary-eyed that evening in 2001 as members of Congress sang God Bless America on the steps of the Capitol. We were brought together as proud, united Americans.

The second event that brought back that neighborhood memory was hearing that our country didn't need a history curriculum based on the 1619 Project but instead, one that was "pro-American, celebrating the truth about our nation's great history." While purporting to be pro-American, that sentiment was a clear message: a curriculum grounded in an African American reality was anti-American. That message justified the feelings of those neighbors who said the flag didn't represent their values.

For those unfamiliar with the 1619 Project, in August 2019, the *New York Times Magazine* published a groundbreaking edition. Every article centered our country's history on the arrival, 400 years earlier, of 20-30 enslaved Africans. Noted journalist Nikole Hannah-Jones used that seminal event to tell our country's history, focusing on the contributions of African Americans throughout America's history. Then, partnering with the Pulitzer Center, the 1619 essay became a free curriculum for classroom teachers.

I have concerns about how our country's history is taught. Using the 1619 Project as the starting place sounded exactly right to me. I thought it would finally tell the actual truth of our nation's history. Hannah-Jones starts her opening essay by saying her Father always flew the American flag proudly in front of their home. But she didn't understand how he could love a country she felt had never loved him. But, after a complete examination of the country's history and deep reflection (remember 'REVEAL, REFLECT, RECALIBRATE'), she ends the essay noting: "We were told once, by virtue of our bondage, that we could never be American. But it was by virtue of our bondage that we became the most American of all." With pride, not only does Hannah-Jones understand her Father's belief in and love for the country, she has proudly staked her own claim as an American. Only to have the essay and project attacked as not 'pro-American' by the highest levels of government and prohibited in the duplicitous and Machiavellian wording and language of a presidential executive order.

I'm torn.

For many, I know what image comes to mind when picturing the all-American boy. I believe I know what comes to mind for many when they think of the American dream.

Try that right now.

What were/are your thoughts? Tell the truth.

In your mind's eye, I don't think that boy has dreadlocks and brown skin. He is white and lives in that suburban house with a well-manicured lawn.

The "American" narrative, that pro-American truth distortion of our history, is still grounded in white skin and white-centered values.

The 'pull yourself up by your bootstraps, equality of opportunity, hard work leads to success' values may be American, but they—like the history that has been taught—are not valid for all.

It's hard for me, and many Black people, to embrace fully the American flag, the flag of a country that doesn't seem to include us. But I am trying. I want to claim my country and feel the sense of pride felt in the aftermath of September 11, 2001. I want to work for a racially just America that reflects the words in those patriotic songs and the country's founding documents.

And I believe more white people today than in our country's history are trying to understand the America that Black people see. I believe more and more are joining the BIPOC community to work toward a racially just, pro-America reality.

I believe we can create an inclusive America stronger than anything envisioned in the 18th century. One without a sole image representing an idealized all-American boy or girl that excludes the diversity of the nation we've become. One where the American dream is not solely defined by a white person—a white family—owning a house. We must determine what a truly democratic economy looks like and how can we— we, the people—ensure everyone succeeds in this all-embracing, new America.

I hope one day, maybe soon, we can all proudly wave that flag.

THE DATE I RECLAIMED THE AMERICAN FLAG.

ORIGINALLY PUBLISHED IN NOVEMBER 2020

November 7, 2020: When I watched TV coverage of election celebrations from Atlanta, New York, Philadelphia, and my city of Washington, DC, I saw liberals and Democrats waving the American flag. BIPOC, LGBTQ, people whose T-shirts and buttons proudly proclaimed who they were and what they valued, people who had been demeaned and insulted, bullied, and dismissed. People who looked like me, people who shared my views and my hopes.

For me, right-wing America, the far-right-wing, had co-opted the American flag. The flag-wavers I usually saw weren't simply those who called themselves conservative but people whose views of what America should be involved in taking away their fellow Americans' rights. They insulted, maligned, minimized, and marginalized anyone whose opinions, skin color, religious beliefs, or families differed from their own. They waved that flag with aggression and superiority. The symbols that represented them—especially the American flag—couldn't represent me.

So, I noticed them... people I can identify with... as they raised and waved that flag, a symbol I had become doubtful would ever represent what I—and they—believed in.

The announcement that Joe Biden was president-elect and Kamala Harris was vice president-elect was met with shouts, cheers, horn honking, and ... flag waving as people celebrated the end of four long years of hatred, lies, and national disgrace. They celebrated the election of a man of integrity who pronounced he would reclaim the soul of America, a man with vision, a leader for all Americans. They celebrated the first Black, the first woman vice president, and even the first, second gentleman. They were joyful, smiling, dancing, high-fiving, and proudly waving our flag. I noticed. I felt the same way: a new lightness and relief at reclaiming America and the American flag as my symbol, a symbol of my country, a country that isn't perfect but one whose days ahead now seem hopeful.

We can make America great... it can live up to its ideals. The president-elect encapsulated America in one word: Possibilities.

Yes.

A More Perfect Union

ORIGINALLY PUBLISHED IN SEPTEMBER 2018

I live in Washington, DC, and for a long time thought my physical location was a big part of what made me a political junkie. The local news is, after all, the national news. But it isn't just location; it is also immediacy. Sometimes, I know, have met, or have seen on the street politicians in the news. This minor familiarity makes them more than just names. And it isn't just proximity; it is also a recognition and an appreciation of how much was sacrificed for me to have the ability to vote, a right that shapes so much of what is reflected in the news.

I can't envision a day without CNN, the *Washington Post*, or the various news alerts on my cell phone. I'm hooked. I have to know what is happening in my world, even when the day's events are troubling. So, as you might expect, I can't imagine not playing an active role in our country's political reality. I simply can't imagine not voting. As the mid-term elections get closer, I wonder if people will vote... and I'm completely baffled and angered by the possibility that people will stay home.

How can you not vote? Particularly African Americans who didn't have the right to vote until 1870, almost a century after this country was founded on the basis that 'all men are created equal.' It was only then that the 15th Amendment to the U.S. Constitution was ratified, giving Black men the ability to vote. When Blacks used that power of the vote and gained a few state offices in the late 1800s, they were struck down. In my home state of Virginia, and in many others, the power brokers of the time then put in place literacy tests and poll taxes, barriers that many could not overcome. In just four years, the number of Black voters in Virginia went from 147,000 in 1901 to only 5,000 by

1905. Even 50 years later, in 1956, when an organization in Richmond started actively registering Blacks to vote, they discovered that only 19% of eligible Black voters were registered. Voter suppression strategies had worked.

Today, hard-fought political gains—post-1965 Voting Rights Act gains—are again being threatened. Just as the election of some Blacks to political offices in post-Civil War America led to efforts to squelch power, so did the election of an African American president. Coordinated efforts, perhaps not as overt as the 1902 Virginia Constitution change that reduced the number of Black voters, but coordinated efforts are being used to lessen the political power of Black Americans.

In recent years, robocalls to voters have announced inaccurately that the polls have closed or named a winner even when voting is still open. States are also moving to structural changes, such as requiring government-issued IDs to vote, a measure that has a disproportionate and potentially long-term effect on communities of color.

But one of the more repugnant strategies was seen in 2018 when the white, Republican gubernatorial candidate in Florida urged his supporters not to "monkey this up," an age-old reference to Black people's presumed animalistic qualities and low intelligence. His opponent was African American. "Don't screw this up" or "Don't mess this up" are everyday expressions that roll off the tongue. His comment to not "monkey this up" is not an everyday expression. It was a clear, pointed, and racialized message to those who consciously and subconsciously continue to see African Americans as less than human. His statement was in no way benign. It was calculated and racist.

I grew up in a time when every new Black elected official was celebrated. My parents and neighbors celebrated Carl Stokes, the first mayor of a major American city, Cleveland, and Richard Hatcher, the mayor of Gary, Indiana. They even celebrated Edward Brooke, the first African American in the United States Senate since Reconstruction, even though soon after his victory, he announced: "I do not intend to be a national leader of the Negro people."

As the number of Black elected officials has grown at the local, state, and national levels, we may have been lulled into thinking we are well-represented. We are not. Currently, there are 47 Black members of the House of Representatives (including two non-voting delegates), 47 out of 435, and three Black U.S. Senators out of 100. There are no Black governors. [Did you know: those of us who live in the nation's capital do not have a voting member of Congress. We have a delegate.]

All of this will change with the November mid-term elections. The question is, in which direction. While on the one hand, I see a heightened sensitivity among many in America to racial injustice, I also see ongoing inequities, many of which can be changed only by those who wield the power of the people—elected officials.

When election day arrives, vote. Elect those who can make this a land in which we truly are working for that 'more perfect union' promised in the Constitution.

* * *

*The 118th Congress that was sworn in in January 2023 includes 60 Black members. There is only one Black governor in the United States as of this writing.

Should a Select Committee Investigate Racism in the U.S.?

ORIGINALLY PUBLISHED IN AUGUST 2022

Like many, I watched the Select Committee to Investigate the January 6th Attack on the U.S. Capitol. I've watched them all, from Chairman Bennie Thompson's opening comments at the first hearing on June 9th, 2022, to the July 21st closing comments from Vice Chair Liz Cheney. The hearings have been riveting, not a bombastic spectacle, but a tempered, dispassionate presentation of what led to the event, what happened on that day, and what has happened since. We are beginning to fully understand how this assault on American democracy unfolded and what would have been the ramifications had it succeeded. I believe we're doing this, in part, so our country might recognize the toxic political partisanship that almost destroyed us, address it, and, hopefully, begin to heal.

Racism, visibly and invisibly, has also divided our country. We're just beginning to see this. So, imagine if we had the same type of examination of slavery, segregation, and the overall impact of racism on America—the same level of thoroughness to examine how people of color have been treated and the effect of that treatment on disparate groups and the country.

How would that story be told?

The January 6th hearings are compelling because real people tell their own stories. You can relate to, even feel, their emotions. Because so much of the foundation of racism happened centuries ago, telling this story will be more difficult, but I think it can still be told.

For example, without video and first-hand accounts, how would the terror of having your land taken and your people exterminated be told? Maybe those living in war-ravaged countries where predators have come to take their land could describe their experience. Could they be modern-day proxies for what happened in America centuries ago? I think so. And coupling those stories with disclosures from people living today who were taken to Indian boarding schools could bring the total trauma of that experience to life.

Without people alive today, how would the committee capture the horrors of being kidnapped, brought to a foreign land, and forced to work from before sunrise to after sunset in atrocious conditions? Perhaps some of those brought to this country in current times as domestic workers and then enslaved by their employers could tell their stories. I know it's not the same, but perhaps hearing those agonized accounts will offer insights.

Then, the committee could listen to real first-hand experiences in *Voices Remembering Slavery: Freed People Tell Their Stories.* These are actual accounts, recorded interviews with the formerly enslaved between 1932 and 1975, and stored at the Library of Congress. But even those accounts may not reveal the complete truth since some suggest that the experience of oppression and fear of white people may have caused some formerly enslaved people to alter their stories to not fully incriminate their oppressors and be punished for telling the truth. Yes, fear even decades after slavery had ended.

While some parts of the story of racism would have to be approximated or told via recordings, that would not be the case in the discussion of Jim Crow laws and the 20th and 21st-century treatment of people of color in America. The reality of disparities in education, health care, housing, the in/justice system, and overall economics could be told by real people today. Some might be elders who were taken out of schools in the 8th grade to work the fields, or soldiers returning from World War II or the Korean War wanting good neighborhoods and housing for their families, or some might be contemporaries, such as the families of those who are now incarcerated for offenses—remember three strikes you're out—that are currently touted as desirable entrepreneurial opportunities and some witnesses might be people simply seeking unbiased appraisals today of the value of their homes or quality public schools for their children.

The truth can be told if America is ready to hear, learn from, and then change... to heal.

Racism is a deep wound that continues to affect our country. A wound/a disease cannot be accurately treated until you know what caused it and then address it correctly. That is what the January 6th committee is attempting to do—find the truth, repair the fissures in our country, and, hopefully, heal.

We've never had a national conversation about race. The closest we've come that I'm aware of is the President's Commission on Race, established by then-President Bill Clinton in 1997. Have you heard of it? It was chaired by noted historian John Hope Franklin and charged with conducting town hall meetings, examining data, and creating solutions to address the racial divide. The intent was correct, and the leadership stellar, but one of the first lessons in racial justice work is that intent and impact are very different. While well-intentioned, I don't believe this commission significantly impacted racial justice. In fact, 25 years later, our inability to examine and discuss race and racial injustice seems to be worsening. Maybe the country wasn't ready in 1997. I'm not so sure that it is now. Still, I know when a group of Texas educators want to refer to slavery as involuntary relocations, that's a clear sign that truth is lacking. Obfuscation and denial continue.

Even in this post-Trayvon Martin, post-Barack Obama, post-George Floyd world of awakening to racial injustice, are we ready for a Congressional Hearing on Racism? I believe, if done correctly and with complete transparency, it would get us closer to the truth, closer to healing, but is America more primed now than it was in 1997? If the Congressional Select Committee on January 6th can be an example, we know that Congress can investigate a travesty against the country and present its findings in a way that compels almost 20 million Americans to watch. We'll just have to wait to see what happens because of all the revelations. If the country can handle the truth about January 6th, learn from it, and then act, maybe it can take the truth about racism.

What Did July Reveal?

I have been told that *1619* by Pulitzer Prize-winning reporter Nikole Hannah-Jones is a long-form journalistic project. I wasn't sure of the correct literary characterization, but what I was, and am certain of, is its profound impact on me.

Jones' revelatory piece centers America's emergence not to 1776, but back even further to 1619, the year the first Africans were brought here. Jones and other writers examine how our country developed and evolved system-by-system, focusing on the Black experience.

She starts *1619* with reflections on her Father and his relationship with the American flag. She shared that her Father always had a huge American flag in the front yard. She couldn't understand why since, in her view, America hadn't treated him well. Then, upon reflection, she realized that it was Black people, including her Father, who had fought most rigorously for the rights America says it holds dear. She wrote:

> "My Father, one of those many black Americans who answered the call, knew what it would take me years to understand: that the year 1619 is as important to the American story as 1776. That black Americans, as much as those men cast in alabaster in the nation's capital, are this nation's true 'founding fathers.' And that no people have a greater claim to that flag than us."

Respecting the flag was just automatic for me, starting in my segregated elementary school. We stood every morning and said the Pledge of Allegiance. My thinking more critically about the flag and what it symbolized started around college. Flags were burned then as a symbol of disagreement with the positions taken by the country. Then, the flag seemed to be adopted by some as a symbol for actions/positions that I didn't support. "Love it or leave it" wasn't what I wanted. I wanted my country to grow, improve, and live up to its founding principles. I didn't want to leave it. I wanted to celebrate it. I just wanted it to be different. The people I saw being celebrated as patriotic as they waved the American flag wanted a different America than I did. Their America seemed to be grounded in racist policies and many other isms that didn't reflect the America I wanted.

Jones' essay crystallized my ambiguity, specifically around the flag. The posts in July were intended to acknowledge all that America, as represented by the flag, hasn't achieved while prompting us to work toward that perfect union.

REFLECT ON THESE QUESTIONS

- Are you aware of any proposals or actions in your city that threaten the voting rights of the BIPOC community? If not, research it to see if you've missed something. If you have, what actions will you take?
- Are you beginning to see evidence of the invisibility of racist policies, practices, and/or behaviors?

NOTES:

AUGUST

While you get into your last summer activities, I want you to think about the odd coincidences of August 28th. On this date in 1955, a Black boy who had just turned fourteen, Emmett Till, was kidnapped, tortured, and lynched in Mississippi. In 1963, on the same day, 250,000 people came to Washington, DC, and participated in the March on Washington for Jobs and Freedom. Forty-five years later, on this same date in 2008, Barack Obama officially accepted the Democratic nomination for President of the United States in Denver, Colorado.

Horror, hope, and pride are associated, for me, with each event. Horror at what happened to Emmett Till, but pride in his mother's ability to show the country what had been done to her son in her hope that the atrocity of what happened to him would lead to change. While most Black Americans were hopeful for the impact of the March on Washington, 63% of Americans in a Gallup poll before the march were fearful of what might happen. And when Barack Obama was named the nominee for president, I felt such pride and hope for this country. Still, my strongest emotion was fear that he would be assassinated before the election.

This month's readings focus on the daily fear and trauma that Black people live with. It's a way of living in America that is not known or experienced by most white Americans. Just imagine that this was your everyday life.

I close the August posts with a personal story on how, like all parents, mine tried to protect me from the ugliness and reality of racial injustice as I grew up in Richmond, Virginia.

"There's a heightened sense of fear and anxiety when you feel like you can't trust the people who've been put in charge to keep you safe. Instead, you see them killing people who look like you. ... Combined with the everyday instances of racism, like microaggressions and discrimination, that contributes to a sense of alienation and isolation. It's race-based trauma."
—Monnica Williams, clinical psychologist, director, Center for Mental Health Disparities, University of Louisville

Racial Trauma is Real

ORIGINALLY PUBLISHED IN FEBRUARY 2023

Just imagine, every day, you are poised for something bad to happen. You may not be conscious of the tension, but it's there. You're primed for a fight or flight. That's part of what it's like to be Black in America.

Sometimes, you're just ready for someone to follow you in a store thinking you're a thief or to disparage a section of town, or offer a backhanded compliment (microaggression) on how articulate you are. But often, you're waiting for the next big shoe to drop.

I've been tense, expecting something terrible—some racially motivated event—since 2012, when Trayvon Martin was killed. The catalyst wasn't just Trayvon Martin; it was the series of lost lives that came after his, but there is no doubt that Trayvon Martin was my ground zero. I experienced his death personally, viscerally. It was hard for me to read the news or watch the coverage. My son and Trayvon were born 366 days apart. When I learned of Trayvon's birthday and the normalcy of that evening when he was killed, I immediately connected my son and Trayvon. My son could have been walking home from the grocery store near our home. Nothing but time, space, and fate caused this to happen to Trayvon and not my son.

While incidents of violence against Black people, especially boys and men, have always been known and discussed in the Black community, it wasn't until the years immediately following Trayvon's murder that we started to regularly see the images. Suddenly, video cameras were everywhere—home and business security cameras, police body cameras, and citizens with their phones. We weren't only hearing about tragedies; we were watching them, a lot of them, one after another.

Imagine, for example, watching violence happen routinely to white women with blonde hair. If you were a blonde woman, maybe you'd choose to wear a wig or dye your hair until the source of the violence was discovered and addressed. As a member of this subset of the white community—blonde and female—you would probably feel confident that the source of the violence would be identified quickly and taken care of.

Now, imagine you are a Black man or boy. You cannot and don't want to camouflage your skin color or race. The causes of much of the violence you face are already known—racism, prejudice, ignorance, and fear. Unlike the anticipated response to the blonde women, there isn't a widespread effort to address the causes of violence against the Black community. In fact, some want to ignore the reasons, like the response to teaching the entirety of our country's racial history. Or the response takes an inordinate time (anti-lynching legislation was first introduced in Congress in 1918 and passed over one hundred years later in 2020 following the televised "lynching" of George Floyd). So, there's little to make the Black community think this violence and trauma will end.

I don't live in fear for myself, primarily because of my age and gender, but I do live in fear for my son. He assures me that he isn't afraid. I hear him, but I believe he subliminally carries this fear daily. He knows his physical presence alone causes some white women to fear him and that they can call the police and say a Black man is threatening them and be believed.

This feeling of being in danger or having a loved one at risk is constant for most Black people. It may not be at the surface of one's day-to-day life, but it's there. According to all that I read, living with stress—and this fear certainly causes stress, acknowledged or unknown—contributes to high blood pressure, heart disease, obesity, and diabetes, all conditions in which Black people are disproportionately represented.

I recently watched the evening news with three friends; two were Black, and two were white. The anchor began to discuss the death of a Black man, Keenan Anderson, after he was tasered by Los Angeles police officers. The video came on. I averted my eyes. Every time I see another incident, the fear for my son increases. The other Black person in the room didn't watch either. I guess we've both seen enough. We can't watch the inhumanity against Black people any longer, but I'm glad our white friends watched. While the images cause me pain, they have revealed our reality to many in white America. But must our continued pain and death be necessary to open eyes, hearts, and minds to the need for change?

The Day ... The Moment

Originally Published in June 2020

On June 19th—Juneteenth—many in the Black community celebrate the end of slavery. In a twisted chain of events, enslaved people in Galveston, Texas, were the last in the country to learn their freedom had been granted. While emancipation was effective on January 1, 1863, Union soldiers didn't bring the message to Texas until June 19, 1865, almost two-and-a-half years later. That was the moment.

Will the murder of George Floyd by Derek Chauvin also be remembered as the moment? Will May 25, 2020, stand as the day when America finally understood racism and bias are real, the tipping point leading to racial justice, not just for Floyd, but for all African Americans?

The image of Chauvin, with his hand casually in his pocket, as he pressed his knee into George Floyd's neck until he died, could be the picture marking a racial epiphany for America. When I watched the videos of Floyd's murder, I thought of the grainy images from a century ago of smiling white families 'enjoying' the prospect of a lynching. In case you missed that, in history, men, women, and children often came out on a Sunday afternoon to be 'entertained' by a human being twisting at the end of a hangman's rope.

"Black bodies swinging in the summer breeze ... Strange fruit hanging from the poplar trees..." sang Billie Holiday in 1939.

The song's lyrics originated as a poem—'Bitter Fruit'—written by Jewish-American writer, teacher, and songwriter Abel Meeropol. He wrote it in 1937 as a protest against lynching. Although fearing reprisal, Holiday sang the piece with specific rules for that part of her

127

performance. There must be reverence. She would close with it; the waiters would stop all service in advance; the room would be in darkness except for a spotlight on her face, and there would be no encore.

Eighty-one years later, was Chauvin—sensing his own limelight—offering a macabre form of sick entertainment and conscious of it? Mesmerizing the crowd, showing his power over George Floyd as he cavalierly murdered an unarmed, handcuffed man? Black oppression is real. Has white America finally got it?

I think—I hope—so. I see and hear a difference in the language used and actions taken. Sadly, the event isn't substantively different from so many in the past, and the marchers with uplifted signs may seem the same. Still, the responses by those in power seem different. I see chiefs of police kneeling in solidarity with peaceful protesters. News commentators acknowledge that most protesters are nonviolent, but agitators have been brought in to foment hate and destruction. I hear elected officials stating the unrest in their cities and states has been brewing for decades as racism and bias have gone unacknowledged and unaddressed. I see Facebook posts asking how white allies can be engaged. People are looking at what happened and why, calling for change.

It is far too early to know where these responses may lead. But I don't recall this level of what seems to be racial understanding being revealed in the past. Are these just platitudes, idle gestures? Maybe. I hope not. I prefer to think there was a confluence of events, a perfect storm. The pandemic with the resulting unemployment of thousands already underemployed. The murder of Ahmaud Arbery in February. Breonna Taylor killed in her home in Louisville in March. The racial profiling of Christian Cooper combined with the killing of George Floyd. All have revealed—powerfully and clearly—racial injustice in America. I feel a difference. I pray this is not merely my hope. This has to be real. America cannot continue as it is.

We know our country has been flawed from its beginning. Founded on racism and bias in favor of wealthy white men. That faulty foundation has remained relatively stable for centuries. The cracks and fissures now seem too large to ignore. We may finally be ready to address the original sin and the decades-long repercussions.

I am fully committed to envisioning and creating a racially just, racially equitable America. The time is now; this is the moment.

* * *

*In 2022, Chauvin was found guilty and sentenced to over 20 years in prison.

The "N" Word, Blackface: Enough!

ORIGINALLY PUBLISHED IN MARCH 2019

A couple of weeks ago, Maryland State Delegate Mary Ann Lisanti admitted to describing Prince George's County, Maryland, as "That 'N' district." After acknowledging she made the statement, she apologized. But when asked by the *Washington Post* if she had ever used the 'N' word, she said, "I'm sure I have... I'm sure everyone has."

Am I that naïve? Is this a regularly used term by everyone? Surely, her 'everyone' doesn't include Black people. And do all white people really use this word casually and routinely?

I know it is popular for some young Black people. It is used throughout certain music lyrics and is sprinkled by some in conversation. Several years ago, there was a notable conversation between Jay Z and Oprah. He said the 'N' word was just a word and that its power came from the intention of the user. That is one view. It's not Oprah's, and it's not mine. I have never said it. When I hear it, it has a harshness. For me, that word evokes hatred, degradation, and Vileness, but then I am more of Oprah's generation than Jay Z's.

When I first heard of Lisanti's comment, I thought her 'everyone' might mean all white people. I hope not and really don't believe that. What I am inclined to believe is that it is an acceptable term among *her* friends and family. In her community, I fear, no one would give a second thought to using it, and no one's head would jerk back to see who said it. 'Everyone' is everyone in her world. That's a problem, a serious one. An elected state official believes that everyone uses the

'N' word. She believes that everyone sees Black people in such a way that Black or African American isn't the term of choice. No, it's 'N,' and with it comes a fully formed narrative about who that person is, along with a recognition that those sentiments reflect what is in her head and in her heart.

As we have recently learned from Virginia officials, racial insensitivity and ignorance are far more rampant than most would like to think. The Virginia Governor and Attorney General both admitted to having been in blackface. The First Lady of Virginia recently offered raw cotton to 13- and 14-year-olds touring the Governor's Mansion so they might think what it would have been like to be a slave (Note: Tobacco was the cash crop for Virginia. Why did she choose to use cotton?) This is not only happening in Virginia, my home state. Before a recent election in Florida, one candidate urged voters "Not to monkey it up."

Just as Ron DeSantis was using this negative, animalistic trope to refer to his black opponent, Lisanti was directly referring to the mostly Black population of Prince George's County. She was not using the 'N' word as a term of endearment or brotherhood, as Jay Z suggested. She was using it as a derogatory reference to the fact that 65% of the residents of the county, according to the last census, are African American. And just as a boutique in Paris didn't care or didn't know how much money Oprah Winfrey had when the salesperson refused to show her a $38,000 handbag, I suspect that Lisanti either didn't know or didn't care that 5 of the 10 wealthiest Black communities in America are in Prince George's County. And at one time, this county was touted as having the largest number of Black millionaires. The color of their skin and what that means or suggests within her value system was the issue, not their economic status.

Lisanti has been censured by the Maryland House of Delegates. They have taken away her subcommittee leadership position, but as of this writing (note the date – March 2019), she still sits as an elected leader in the state of Maryland. Governor and Mrs. Northam still occupy the Governor's Mansion in Richmond. Mark Herring is still the Attorney General of Virginia, and, even with his coarse comment, last

November, Ron DeSantis was elected Governor of Florida. And these aren't just the recent ones. They're just the ones we know about.

What does having these leaders in Virginia, Maryland, or Florida mean for the people of their states? Whose needs do they understand? Which citizens do they fight for? Who do they see as the contributors to the success and promise of their states? Who do they believe are the dregs that detract from their states? Your word choices and actions reflect what is in your head and your heart, and they have significant ramifications, consciously and unconsciously.

I do not believe you can fully represent the needs of people you demean, people whom you do not value.

Elected officials who belittle cannot be removed from office for callousness or ignorance. They have done nothing against the law. They have, however, revealed their inability to represent the needs of their entire constituency. When that has been shown by the words they say and the actions they take, they should apologize, and they should resign. That—perhaps—might help them regain, at a minimum, some integrity.

* * *

P.S. Mary Ann Lisanti lost her seat in the Maryland House of Delegates in the 2022 election.

Never a Victim

Originally Published in March 2018

Friends often ask me, "How could you have grown up in segregated Richmond, Virginia, in a stark separate-but-equal environment without witnessing overt signs of segregation?"

Their question stems from a truth I've shared with them: I have no memory of seeing whites-only and colored-only water fountains. No time when I was denied access to restaurants. No riding in the back of the bus. None of that. As a child, I had no understanding that my world was defined by race. People don't believe me when I tell them this, but it's true.

Some suggest that my mind has blocked negative images or memories.

I don't believe that. I think a far more powerful explanation exists: Edna Charity Lucas and Howard Edward Lucas, my parents. In hindsight, I know they went to great lengths, as many Black parents did, to see that I never felt any level of second-class citizenship. Another thing: they did not talk about discrimination, at least not where I could hear. I think that was important in shaping my reality.

My Mom would pack a delicious lunch for our road trip to visit family in New York. Then, halfway there, my Dad would pull the car into a roadside picnic area. No one commented that we were doing this because we couldn't eat in restaurants along the way. My parents simply pulled out our lunch, put a tablecloth on the wooden picnic table, and we played games—looking for cars with license plates from different states—as we ate and enjoyed what we now consider quality family time. And when my Dad stopped at the Esso, now Exxon, service station to buy gas, we would go to the bathroom. I didn't think anything of it. But his lifelong loyalty to Exxon was born from that company being the first to let Blacks use the restroom facilities in their service stations, a reality I learned from books, not from my Dad telling me.

There was one childhood incident that was probably exposure to separate-but-equal, but I didn't know it then. My Mom and I had entered the train station to travel to visit relatives. I remember skipping ahead toward a seat. My Mom took my hand and gently directed me to another area. I now suspect she led me to the 'colored' area. No conversation, just a subtle re-direction. I don't recall even noticing it at the time. The possibility/probability of this being a separate-but-equal memory only surfaced as an adult when friends questioned my experience of segregation as a child. Again, the important point was there was no preamble as I was being led away from where I was headed. At no time did anyone tell me that there was something I couldn't do or someplace I couldn't go.

Of course, I lived in a segregated neighborhood. I attended a segregated school but didn't know I was being denied anything. My community was lovely, and I never felt as supported in any educational environment as I did in that school. My point, simply, is that the harshness of segregation as a reality that makes someone superior to you never consciously entered my psyche. Was this level of insulation by my parents positive, or did it cause me to have an unrealistic sense of the world? I'm not sure.

All I know is that when whites entered my world via integration, I didn't fear them, nor did I dislike them. I did not feel that they were the persecutors and I was the victim. I think that is the most important point. Victims are powerless. Being a victim wears you down. You are continually looking for injustice, looking for where/how you have been wronged. It causes physical and mental stress. I am not saying that prejudice has not been a part of my life. Of course, it has, but that is not the frame I start with every day. Whites had, and have, more power than I do, but I have always approached my interactions with them as equals, even as a child. Now, as an adult, injustice surrounds me in the governmental processes and structures that have, with intentionality, disadvantaged me and my community. It is the media that often portray negative images of Black people. It was in the rhetoric of the President of the United States. It is truly in the air I breathe. But I am still not a victim.

My parents wisely and bravely chose to deflect—but not deny—segregation's impact on me even as they raised me within its confines. They dealt with the reality of it while telling me I could do anything I wanted. As I work for racial understanding and justice, I recognize I was raised to be a daughter of the dream, never to be a victim.

What Did August Reveal?

I've heard it. Maybe you have, too. Unless I live with greater health consciousness, I will face this or that health condition. My body is simply predisposed to develop certain illnesses or diseases. The growing study of genetics reveals the physical challenges that may become our reality based simply on who we are.

For many years, that thinking was confined to physical health, but more and more, it is associated with psychological health as well.

I certainly know how hopes and dreams are passed on generation to generation. Sometimes, they aren't even fully articulated; you just know.

I also know how hate and prejudice can be passed from one generation to the next.

An increasing number of social scientists believe that trauma can live not only in our brains but also in our cells. The belief is that unresolved trauma can live in our DNA, affecting us for years and our progeny for generations.

Post-traumatic slave syndrome is a term coined by Dr. Joy DeGruy Leary in 2005. It is a condition that describes the internalized racism, fear, and loss of self-esteem that Dr. Leary attributes to slavery and the post-slavery decades of oppression and degradation. PTSS is not yet acknowledged by the American Psychiatric Association, but many believe this theory merits reflection and consideration.

And the impact of stress on our physical and mental health has long been recognized. According to a November 1, 2022 article (updated 3/8/23) from the American Psychological Association: "Stress affects all systems of the body including the musculoskeletal, respiratory, cardiovascular, endocrine, gastrointestinal, nervous, and reproductive systems." Stress is a killer.

Black people started their lives in America in extraordinarily stressful situations. That stress continued in the Jim Crow and Civil Rights eras as Black Americans negotiated the delicate and sometimes unstated relationship they must maintain with whites to survive. Today, cell phone videos and news reports have shown the multiple, everyday situations that continue to put the lives of Black people in danger.

REFLECT ON THESE QUESTIONS

- Do you believe that racial trauma is real? Why or why not?
- What do you think when you hear the belief that Black men or boys are victimizers? How do you respond? What do you say about "that other side of town" or when you hear others mention it in that fashion?

NOTES:

SEPTEMBER

September is the time to go back to school or think about education, even if schooling is long behind you.

Education is often at the center of conversations about racial justice, starting with the need for equitable access to quality education. During times of enslavement up to today, educational opportunities have been viewed as pivotal for success. While research will support the need for quality education, it also shows that education alone is insufficient. For example, deeply rooted biases continue to make job candidates whose names suggest they are African American fall lower on the list of candidates regardless of qualifications.

Today's education debate seems to be focused on what books should be in school libraries and what aspects of our country's racial history should be taught in schools.

When our racial history is not taught in schools, we become self-learners, often with significant knowledge gaps or misinterpretations of events and leaders. REVEALED is intended to fill some of those information voids and to encourage the practice of lifelong learning.

"It's a privilege to learn about racism instead of experiencing it your whole life." —Ahmednur Ali, Scientific Lead, Editor of Health Systems Evidence

School Segregation: Not All Negative

Originally Published in September 2017

The first day of school is always exciting. I'm sure mine was no different when I walked into Albert V. Norrell Elementary School. Even though Brown v. Board of Education had struck down separate-but-equal schooling, my education started in an all-Black school environment. I suspect I didn't notice. All the people in my world were Black. Back then, we were all Negroes—in my family, in my neighborhood, at my church, and now at my school. Nothing new.

At the time, nationally and in Richmond, Virginia, where I lived, people argued whether separate school systems were inherently unequal and whether Black students were disadvantaged by this practice. In many ways, the evidence was clear. We received hand-me-down books from the white schools, our science labs, if we had them, had outdated equipment, and the school facilities had only marginal upkeep.

But there was one significant difference. Everyone was fully dedicated to the students' success in that all-Black environment. From the janitorial crew to the cafeteria team, the entire faculty, all the way to Mrs. Ethel Overby, our principal (the first Black woman ever named to be a principal in the Richmond school system), they were all willing to do whatever it took to nurture our desire to learn and to give us every possible learning opportunity they could. This reality was a powerful counterbalance to the deficits in the system.

I don't believe that Black students experience that degree of total commitment to their success anymore. Now, don't get me wrong. I am not saying that teachers and administrators don't want to see their students succeed. I believe that most do. But put simply, I also think that unconscious bias looms large in the education system. Far too many have bought into ideas—preconceptions—about the pathology of Black families, the inability of Black boys to focus, the myth of laziness, and so on. You know the stereotypes as well as I do.

I remember being surrounded by a cocoon of love and support. I can still remember the pride felt as I stood at school assemblies for the singing of *Lift Every Voice and Sing*, the Negro National Anthem. I knew I could do anything I set my mind to because everyone told me I would be successful. And the actions of everyone around me were intended to open the doors to success and to help me walk through them.

The older I get and reflect on the current state of America, the better I understand my Father's comment that integration was the best thing that happened to Black people and the worst.

Choosing a College was a Black or White Decision

Originally Published in October 2017

When it was time to start thinking about colleges, my parents took me on the typical college tour trip. We didn't go too far from my hometown of Richmond. We visited Hampton University, Virginia State, Fisk in Nashville, and North Carolina Central—all HBCU (Historically Black Colleges and Universities) network members.

Predominantly white schools were also in the mix, having only recently become a significant option for Black students. Some rose to the top from stories from recent high school grads who returned to share their experience. I learned of others from my high school quarterback boyfriend, who was aggressively recruited by many white schools nationwide. When it came time to make that important decision, I chose the College of William and Mary in Williamsburg, Virginia, my boyfriend's choice.

It is interesting to note the reaction that that decision elicited then and now. While my parents were not enamored of the boyfriend, they were of my college choice. At the time, my parents, their friends, and every adult with whom I shared the decision were proud. Virginians knew William and Mary liked to refer to itself as the Ivy League of the South. It was, and is, a small state school with a well-regarded reputation for academic excellence. Being accepted into William and Mary was prestigious for a white student. Acceptance was regarded as even more extraordinary for a Black student. At that time, just a handful of Black students attended. The first was accepted in 1967, two years before my freshman class.

When people learn that I graduated from William and Mary, the reaction is characteristically divided by race. White people, particularly white Virginians, nod their heads positively. Usually, this fact elevates me in their hierarchy of intellectual excellence. Many Black people, on the other hand, shake their heads questioningly. Why did I forego an education grounded in the richness of Black culture at an HBCU to attend predominately white William and Mary? They sometimes ask outright: "Did you get a scholarship?" And when I answer, "No," they either ask me, "Then why did you go there?" or they silently wonder.

The answer has many layers, but at its core, you must consider the times.

My grades were excellent. While not in the top ten of my high school graduating class, I was in the top 15, a member of the National Honor Society, and active in everything from student government to the school yearbook. It was never said to me, but I had been groomed to be one of the first. I knew I was expected to walk through doors as they opened for Blacks. Attending William and Mary was one such door. It was seen as a stepping stone, especially in Virginia, to other career opportunities that would not have been possible just a few short years previously. I sincerely felt my responsibility was to accept when William and Mary accepted me.

Now, in hindsight, the adult me has regretted this decision. College choices back then truly were black or white. I can think of no school at the time which was well-integrated. While I received an excellent education, I do not have rich memories of campus camaraderie or Greek life in a sorority's sisterhood.

Even though the student body voted me onto the homecoming court three out of my four years (the first Black homecoming princess at W&M), I've only returned to homecoming twice. And while I made a few good friends and have no recollection of racism while there, overall, when I think back on college, there is just an emptiness, an experience devoid of the oh-so-important social fabric of college life.

I know my life's trajectory would have been quite different had I made another choice. Better? I'll never know.

* * *

*Since then, I attended the 50th anniversary of my college graduation in 2023.

The Ruse, the Governor, and Critical Race Theory

ORIGINALLY PUBLISHED IN FEBRUARY 2022

The latest reminder of the centrality and primacy of the white worldview happened for me on January 15, 2022, the day Glenn Youngkin was inaugurated as the 74th governor of Virginia. While I haven't lived in Virginia for a long time, it is my home state. I wanted to hear what the new governor had to say.

Not far into his inaugural address, he said, "We will remove politics from the classroom." Attendees jumped to their feet. The sentiment that parents, not the government, should control what is taught in schools—particularly regarding racial history—pushed this never-elected-to-any-office candidate into the Virginia Governor's Mansion. Then he continued, "We will teach all of our history, the good (here he paused) ... and the bad." The crowd sat, seemingly deflated.

Stop. Rewind. Had he actually said that? Yes, those were his words. I wrote them down; I was so surprised. Was there some chance he had thought about it and decided to do the right thing? In his inaugural address, was he ready to signal, no, actually state, that Virginia was not only going to take down Confederate statues, Virginia would also teach the completeness of its history and that of the country?

No, of course not. Upon reflection, how could I be so naïve? Hopeful, I guess that he had thought deeply about his earlier position, understood another side, and decided to make a significant turnaround in his first public address as governor. Yes, I was naively hopeful.

Youngkin's remarks were simply political theater. He said those words just before issuing Executive Order Number One (2022):

> "Inherently divisive concepts, like Critical Race Theory and its progeny, instruct students to only view life through the lens of race and presumes that some students are consciously or unconsciously racist, sexist, or oppressive and that other students are victims."

It goes on to read,

> "The Superintendent of Public Instruction shall review all policies within the Department of Education to identify those that promote inherently divisive concepts. Such policies shall be ended."

And he knew he had the right person to carry out this directive. I checked. As Superintendent of Public Instruction, he had named the former Wyoming State Superintendent of Schools, a person who had been very public in her opposition to teaching Critical Race Theory.

Race is the lens through which many, including Glenn Youngkin, view life. It energized his campaign and was his out-of-the-gate issue as governor.

Race used to sit quietly in the corner, but not anymore. Many, including Youngkin, want to put it back in its place—invisible, undiscussed, unaddressed.

For our country to truly achieve its founding promise, we must understand and address our history. It is that history that has made America what it is today. History has been taught from the perspective of white people who control textbooks and decisions about curricula. Our country's history has been whitewashed and sanitized to glorify whites while demeaning or completely ignoring other races.

Just think about the number of people who had never heard of the Tulsa massacre until *Watchmen* streamed on HBO in 2019 or the number who'd never heard of the Tuskegee syphilis study until the use of Black men as research subjects was revealed in 2020 as the root of some African Americans' concern about COVID vaccinations, or others learning—this year—about Emmett Till through the recent ABC series *Women of the Movement*. I am glad that racial history is being revealed through art and the news, but it should be taught in the classroom, not something one can choose to watch, but in-school subject matter required to be learned.

Youngkin and others claim that they want to avoid the divisiveness caused by teaching what they refer to as Critical Race Theory is simply a smokescreen. In fact, the current approach to teaching our country's history focused on the individual exceptionalism of a few but not on the racially motivated actions of many or on the racist federal, state, and local policies and societal practices that have shaped this country, contributes to ignorance, an ignorance that feeds racial hostility and separation.

Remember Dr. Martin Luther King's reminder, "History will have to record that the greatest tragedy of this period of social transition was not the strident clamor of the bad people, but the appalling silence of the good people." Speak up when your government is doing the wrong thing.

Beyond Data... We Find Humanity

Originally Published in May 2019

In 2019, I finished my second year co-teaching a course on philanthropy and racial equity. Here's the remarkable part: the students—all graduate students in public policy—reported that they had never had a course on racial equity. They were required to learn about economic practices, statistical procedures, and, broadly, ethics, public management, and creating public policy. Like others on racial equity, my course is an elective at this university. It took me a while to figure out why I was bothered by this. Finally, I got it. I looked for and found the JFK quote in the back of my mind. He said: "I know few significant questions of public policy which can safely be confided to computers. In the end, the hard decisions inescapably involve imponderables of intuition, prudence, and judgment." Where is the balance between empirical data and experience? Where does humanity enter? How is the data about disproportionate outcomes by race revealed? Where was the judgment that Kennedy referenced?

When I pointed this out, a colleague cautioned that it is the research base that appeals to students. The students drawn to this campus want to create policies driven by data. I agree data is invaluable in developing sound public policies. But I believe a large realm of facts isn't being considered. A full exploration will occur only by consciously examining what has contributed to racially inequitable public policies. For that to happen, racial equity education must be in the public policy curriculum, not as an elective but as a requirement.

I heard noted author and academic Robin DiAngelo talk about white privilege a few years ago. Midway through her remarks, she commented that one aspect of white privilege is never having to understand racial inequity. She noted that most people will go through college, graduate programs, law school, or medical school without taking a race, racial equity, or racial justice course. She noted that although few are taught this topic, many believe they understand the issues. How can they? Her question and mine is how is that knowledge acquired? Why do so many people believe they understand racial equity without being taught this? It seems they think of it as a lesson in politeness. As long as they treat people respectfully, there will be no inequity. That's not true. In fact, the most detrimental inequities are those embedded in public policy. This has to be academically taught, not casually learned.

It is incumbent upon public policy analysts and practitioners to delve beyond merely presenting aggregated data. We must ask questions to find answers (and solutions). Why are there more people of color incarcerated than white people? Why are the educational outcomes for Black and brown people worse than those for white people? What zoning policies have disproportionately placed more halfway houses in communities of color? What policies and incentives enable more economic growth in certain communities than in others? How is the schedule of actions as basic as street cleaning or bulb replacement in streetlights determined from community to community, and how does it have a racial component?

Your analysis will stop before it reaches the crux if you're not thinking about racial equity. You're unlikely to discern disproportionate impact based on race unless you look. And without being primed to the possibility, you are unlikely to look. A policy might appear race-neutral when it's not.

It's noteworthy that I'm co-teaching this course at Georgetown University. I only mention that because Georgetown has been in the news lately both for acknowledging its role in perpetuating the sale of enslaved Africans and for the vote by the student body to charge an additional attendance fee to create a reparations fund for the descendants of those enslaved people. It's commendable that institutions of higher learning, like Georgetown and my alma mater, the College of William and Mary, are addressing historical, racially driven wrongs.

That lens on past actions is important, but without intentionality and probing, we might miss the wrongs of the present. It took me a minute to see the potential impact in my academic backyard. Not requiring public policy students to learn about racial inequity doesn't seem like a good policy.

What are you missing in your backyard?

TOYS AREN'T JUST PLAYTHINGS

ORIGINALLY PUBLISHED IN DECEMBER 2018

When I was a young girl in the late 1950s, I loved dolls. Lined up on my bed were baby dolls and dolls supposed to be my age and, eventually, even grown-up ones, like Barbie. I loved dressing them up, combing their hair, and having endless conversations with them. But there was a problem.

None of these dolls looked like me. Not one.

My doll-playing years happened just a little over a decade after the groundbreaking research of psychologists Drs. Mamie and Kenneth Clark. In 1947, they released their study showing that Black children as young as three—when given two dolls, identical except for skin and eye color, almost invariably chose a white doll as the one they liked better or wanted to play with. Even though the Black children had the choice of a brown doll that looked like them, they still preferred the white doll. The Clarks concluded that these children had already internalized an unconscious belief that white was better.

The Clark doll research of decades ago and even more recent studies show that children as young as three have a sense of racial identity and hierarchy. This important research points to the impact of all the other messages these children receive—overtly and subtly—about Black and white people.

While my parents couldn't easily find dolls resembling me, today's parents don't have that problem. They have a plethora to choose from. Finding one that racially resembles a child—almost any child—is no longer difficult. Children today see a rainbow of skin colors in dolls, action figures, and Crayon colors labeled 'flesh.' Not only are characters racially diverse in the animated cartoons they watch but also in the books they read. Merchandising and media today seem to reflect the literal complexions of America.

As parents or the adults in children's lives, we know that toys aren't just playthings, items to entertain. We have learned that from all the child development research we consume as we try to be our children's best parents (and grandparents). We know toys are important in shaping how children see and negotiate the world.

Knowing this, we make conscious decisions when buying toys or educational gifts. We want our children's learning to be enhanced by these gifts. When selecting them, I wonder if most parents think about the messages they send about race and how they value people who don't look like them. Consider this comment from Jennifer Richeson, a Yale University social psychologist:

> "In some ways, it's super simple. People learn to be whatever their society and culture teaches them. We often assume that it takes parents actively teaching their kids for them to be racist. The truth is that unless parents actively teach kids not to be racists, they will be. This is not the product of some deep-seated, evil heart that is cultivated. It comes from the environment, the air all around us."

We can and should use the occasion of gift-giving to demonstrate to our children what we value.

I don't believe diversity alone fights racism in the world. Still, by celebrating diversity, those of us who influence children help to instill in them a bias toward a belief that all men and women are created equal. And that is a valuable gift we should want our children to have, right? That is an essential step toward valuing and promoting racial equity.

So, on the next gift-giving occasion, as you think about what to give the children in your life, celebrate who they are and who their friends are. Help them see the beauty, humanity, and intelligence in people who look like them and those who don't. While we don't want our Black children to have a childhood bedroom that looks like mine with all white dolls, we also don't want white children to have that bedroom either.

WHAT DID SEPTEMBER REVEAL?

Sadly, the United States has a history of denying quality educational opportunities to Black people. That history started with the arrival of enslaved Africans.

I believe the United States is the only country with a history of anti-literacy laws. Those laws prevented teaching enslaved people to read and write. Today, even in Afghanistan, where girls are denied an education beyond the primary grades, they learn to read. The fact that enslaved people were kept from learning to read and write underscores the importance attached to education. The enslavers and the enslaved recognized the power that comes with learning.

Here's a little bit of a history lesson. After the end of the Civil War, the Freedmen's Bureau, which was intended to help the formerly enslaved, established schools, but the Bureau only lasted until 1872. For years, outside of the Black community, white churches, and missionaries, there was little attention to the education of Black children.

In 1912, through a friendship between Julius Rosenwald, one of the founders of Sears, Roebuck and Company and *Booker T. Washington, thousands of schools were built for Black children: 4978 in 15 states. This was a private undertaking, not an effort by states or the federal government.

The federal government entered the education arena significantly with the GI Bill following World War II. In 1947, approximately 49% of those entering college were veterans, largely due to the GI Bill enabling families that had never been able to afford college to have that opportunity. Of the over 1 million Black Americans who served in the war, and with all of the instant information at our fingertips due to technology, try to find out how many former African American soldiers were able to utilize the GI Bill's educational benefit. I couldn't. Most, if not all, colleges and universities in the South would not admit Black students.

Historically Black Colleges and Universities were overwhelmed by the volume of requests. So, on paper, a benefit for all who served in the war became another benefit for white Americans.

The Supreme Court came into the national education conversation with the 1954 Brown v. Board of Education decision in which separate-but-equal educational facilities, etc., were deemed unconstitutional.

With the recent Supreme Court decisions on affirmative action and student loans, along with the multiple states across the country that are banning the teaching of the comprehensive history of the country, many feel that educational opportunity and quality education for all is being set back. The posts for September were intended to remind the reader of another area of disparity: education. Educational equity has never been a reality in America, but it can be.

* * *

*Booker T. Washington was an African American educator who focused on self-help. In 1881, Washington was named the head of what was to become Tuskegee University.

REFLECT ON THESE QUESTIONS

- Did you attend a segregated school (remember: it's not only schools with Black students that were/are segregated)? Whatever the racial composition of your school, what impact did that experience have on your racial views?
- Do you know, really know what Critical Race Theory is? What do you want taught at your child or grandchild's school about our country's racial history? Have you made your views known?

NOTES:

OCTOBER

Increasingly, in October, I think of Indigenous People's Day. In 1934, Congress originally proclaimed Columbus Day, and in 1937, the country started celebrating Christopher Columbus and his "discovery." In 1992, Berkeley, California, started celebrating Indigenous People's Day on the 500th anniversary of Columbus arriving on this soil. As racial consciousness grew, there was a growing understanding that this land could not have been discovered in 1492. People already lived here who celebrated the land and its richness, and it was from those Indigenous Peoples that the land was ultimately stolen. In 2021, President Joe Biden officially proclaimed Indigenous People's Day.

The posts this month should remind you that change is possible. Sometimes, it takes decades for the false truth or false idol to be recognized. Just as vistas become clearer after the leaves have fallen or a person's identity is revealed once the Halloween mask is removed, our minds can be opened to see the world more clearly.

> "I alone cannot change the world,
> but I can cast a stone across the waters
> to create many ripples."
> —Mother Teresa

I Am My Brother's Keeper. What About You?

ORIGINALLY PUBLISHED IN MAY 2020

"With enough butter, anything is good," said noted chef Julia Child. I agree, in moderation, that is. Throughout my lifetime, Land O'Lakes has been my family's preferred brand of butter. If that hadn't been the case, I might have missed the tweet from Edgar Villanueva, lauding the company for removing what he called a "racist Native American image." The image of that bright yellow packaging of the Land O'Lakes butter container caught my eye in my Twitter feed.

Edgar Villanueva is a member of the Lumbee tribe of North Carolina. I point that out because unless you are a member of the affronted group, it is sometimes difficult to see racial offenses. The young Native woman who, until February 2020, was centered on the Land O'Lakes package offended him. Even within the oppressed group, the stereotype is sometimes missed. Think how often you have read about Natives saying that the Indian-related names of sports teams are not slurs. I suspect that, like many, they have internalized their own oppression, a condition in which marginalized groups accept what the dominant society believes about them. They live and breathe the same media messages as everyone else. Sometimes, they don't even see the racism, at least not immediately. It often takes someone to point out the stereotypes and their impact: an Edgar Villanueva, for example.

A few years ago, at the height of the conversation about the name of the football team in my city, Washington, DC, I attended a seminar at the National Museum of the American Indian. "From Tarzan to

Tonto" explored stereotypes as distinct and ubiquitous from the savage Indian warrior to the beautiful—and submissive—Indian maiden (the logo of Land O'Lakes). The images are everywhere; most of us just don't see them. And when we do, we think many are benign. But as I know, and you probably do too, any image that reinforces negative characteristics, particularly without a counterweight of accurate depictions, is not benevolent.

If you are of a certain age, you probably grew up watching Western movies or Western-themed television shows. The Indian was either attacking the white settlers or was the humble, often monosyllabic, sidekick to the white star. All these images planted in you... specific thoughts and 'truths' about Native peoples.

Never did you routinely see images portraying the viciousness of white settlers as they took over the land of the Natives. Or the inhumanity of the U.S. government forcing Indian children into residential schools with the explicit purpose: 'kill the Indian in him and save the man.'

Today, without the periodic attention given to the names of sports teams, I suspect most rarely think about Native populations. American Indians are perceived as historical, a people of the past. And, largely, they almost are—they were separated, their land taken, their cultural dances and religious ceremonies prohibited by law. Their sense of self nearly obliterated by a country intent on their annihilation or, certainly, their total assimilation. Without the somewhat recent convening of multiple tribes to protest the Keystone Pipeline,* many people may not have thought about Native populations in any sense of the present. I am thinking about Native peoples ... now. It's recent, though, a new reality for me.

Sticks and stones—their weight over generations—hurt not only our bones but our souls. And a picture, negative to race or creed—whether intentionally or inadvertently—does have a power greater than a thousand words. Be the change you want to see in the world.

* * *

*The Keystone Pipeline is a controversial oil pipeline system in Canada and the United States, commissioned in 2010 and owned by TC Energy. An oil spill would threaten the water supply of many Native populations.

Black and Native

ORIGINALLY PUBLISHED IN JULY 2020

I comment through my African American lens in all my *Daughters of the Dream* posts. That is who I am. That is how I identify. In truth, however, my maternal side of the family is primarily Native members of the Chickahominy Tribe of Virginia. I have known this all my life, but it mostly went unacknowledged. The federal government did not recognize the tribe until 2018. But more importantly, in many ways, it was also unrecognized by my family.

Using Ancestry.com, I watched the evolution of the racial identity of my maternal grandparents. On early census documents, my grandmother was noted as Indian, full-blooded, as the saying goes. My maternal grandfather was noted as Mulatto, which he was, by the definition of that term, mixed Indian and white. Then they both become Mulatto, along with their children, of course. Subsequent census documents list them as colored, then Negro, then Black.

My Mother and her siblings were raised as African American. Perhaps my grandparents had internalized the negativity the white, dominant population associated with being Native. The only time I can remember my Mother celebrating her Native heritage was when she casually commented one Thanksgiving that there was no need to observe this holiday (even though she did). "It was just the beginning of white people taking Indians' land," she said.

Now, I have started the journey of celebrating all of me.

Just as I would not overlook a racist image of an African American or a racist comment about one, I am becoming more attuned to my Native roots and culture. For years, I have recognized the racism in the names of some sports teams. But when conversations turned to the looting following the murder of George Floyd, how many of us thought about the original looters, those who took the land of the Native peoples in this country?

Native and Black are both a part of who I am.

But what about those identities that are not a part of you or me? Just because it is not our identity, racism cannot be ignored. Racism hurts all of us. As Martin Luther King said, "There comes a time when silence is betrayal." The racial mosaic of those who continue to march and speak out against police brutality and racism six weeks after the murder of George Floyd gives me hope. An increasing number of Americans seem to believe—truly believe—we are our brother's keeper.

When BIPOC Becomes Camouflage

Originally Published in September 2021

Black, Indigenous, People of Color (BIPOC). When I first learned this term, it made me happy. I had accepted, but not fully embraced, POC, but finally, Indigenous Peoples were being included explicitly in language and in conversations about racially oppressed/marginalized groups. For me, the term "POC" had now morphed to be linguistically inclusive of a group often forgotten. That was good, and, yes, that was my only thought. The positive.

That was then. This is now. The more I hear the term, the more it bothers me. Here's why.

You'll remember that death numbers were presented in the aggregate at the beginning of the COVID pandemic. We saw the disproportionate impact on distinct communities, particularly Black, Hispanic/Latinx, and Indigenous populations, only after examining race and ethnicity. Once the COVID numbers were disaggregated by race, we knew who was most affected, and specific outreach to those communities began.

Now, I believe aggregated BIPOC data is being used as camouflage. Data must be broken down by race and ethnicity to reveal racial reality.

Recently, a vendor (in the investment banking industry) with whom a colleague was doing business was asked about hiring people of color. Proudly, the company shared its BIPOC numbers but, when asked, declined to disaggregate them by race, saying such an action was against company policies. Huh? Why would a vendor refuse such a request?

I checked the stats for that industry. According to the first site in my Google search, 69.6% of investment bankers are white, 11.4% each for the Asian and Hispanic/Latinx communities, 5.3% are Black, 2% unknown, and .3% are American Indian or Alaska Native. I suspect that, for the vendor being considered, the Black community and the Indigenous community also would not be well-represented, if at all, in their BIPOC data. I believe the vendor declined, knowing the details would show a dearth of Black people in upper-level positions.

Believe me, I intend not to deny opportunities to any non-white community. I celebrate those inroads and appreciate the solidarity of fostering a BIPOC community. PERIOD. Hard stop. I simply want transparency in who is being hired. And, where disproportionality is revealed, like in investment banking, I want us to acknowledge it, examine why it occurs, and address it. We can't handle a problem until we know it exists. That is the invisibility, or shielding, of racism.

As with COVID, we can gain the same clarity by asking employers to break down the details of their BIPOC (or POC) data. And, then, we can do what it takes to grow employment opportunities and hire people not represented or underrepresented within those industries. In the meantime, let's not be lenient on employers who won't disaggregate data. Take your business somewhere else.

Non-smoker | Antiracist: A Parallel Path to Racial Equity

ORIGINALLY PUBLISHED IN OCTOBER 2019

Were you ever a smoker? I was.

The recent news stories about the dangers of e-cigarettes have made me think about that time in my life.

I grew up in Virginia, a major tobacco-growing state. In fact, it was only recently that marijuana pushed tobacco to number two on the list of Virginia's cash crops. When I was growing up, Richmond was home to the Philip Morris Tobacco Company. A huge, cigarette-shaped edifice, with the logos of Marlboro and other top brands plastered over the structure, hovered outside the main plant alongside U.S. Route 95, a major north-south highway. It was iconic. Everyone could see it. Philip Morris was a significant employer in the area and even gave free cigarettes to employees. Every October until 1984, Richmond acknowledged its cash crop with an enormous parade, the Tobacco Festival Parade. Frank Sinatra was the parade's Grand Marshall in 1948. It was just that big.

My parents smoked. Their friends smoked. Not only was there no stigma to smoking when I was growing up, it was almost expected. But I may not have smoked if I hadn't had a cigarette-smoking roommate in college who looked incredibly sophisticated and just plain cool as she held a cigarette.

Now, I haven't had a cigarette in almost forty years.

165

One day, a few months after I quit, I came into my apartment and realized just how foul it smelled. The stench of smoke was not clear to me until weeks after I stopped. It clung to me and had been there all along. I just didn't know it.

So why am I telling you this? There is a stench to racism, too. Many just haven't been able to "smell" it until recently. Now, some—a growing number—are seeing it, understanding it, and quitting.

Yes, I see the trajectory of non-smoking in America as similar to the path to understanding and addressing racism.

Here goes.

Almost 72% of American men and 55% of women smoked in 1980 when I stopped. Smoking was embedded in our world. No one really thought much about it. It was almost invisible, like racism, particularly structural racism.

I was too young to notice when Congress first warned of the dangers of smoking in 1965. I was nominally aware when the health warning appeared on cigarette packages and when cigarette advertising was banned from television in 1970, but I didn't stop smoking then. The dangers of it were still too far removed. I began to pay attention when a family member died from lung cancer. Yet it took the proliferation of messages in the popular media and personal situations to get me—and many like me—to finally stop smoking. That constant drumbeat, the layering of messages from many people and sources, finally made me quit and led to widespread public policies like the smoking bans we see today.

This is the same path to understanding and addressing structural racism and implicit bias.

We are at the point in our nation's history where we are beginning to recognize the dangers of racism. Many reports have been released that speak to its deleterious impact not just on people of color but on all people. I don't believe that the U. S. Surgeon General has released such a report. Still, the American Academy of Pediatrics has cited racism as a "socially transmitted disease, passed down through generations, leading to the inequities observed in our population today." The American Academy of Pediatrics is not alone; group after group offers societal warnings. They are becoming cumulative, and they are becoming mainstream.

I needed personal situations along with research data to push me to stop smoking. Individual instances of structural racism and implicit bias directly affect many in America. And while the effect of smoking on me wasn't known any further than my family and close friends, cell phone videos and social media are broadening the sharing and the impact of personal stories of racism. We know their names.

Americans still smoke—16.7% of men and 13.6% of women—but you notice smokers and wonder why they are doing something so detrimental to their health and the quality of the air we breathe.

And we are noticing racism more. It is important that questions were raised about the recent sentencing of a white woman, Felicity Huffman,* in comparison to that of a black woman, Kelly Williams-Bolar,* both mothers seeking better educational opportunities for their children. It wasn't until recently that such a racial equity lens would have been applied.

Like smoking, it is unlikely that racism will ever be totally gone from society. Still, we must remain vigilant and continue to notice, talk about the dangers, and act, individually and societally, against it. It's not enough for you to just see your own racially-charged actions and quit, so to speak; you must encourage others to stop as well. You must use your voice to be a part of that needed plethora of messages. As Ibram Kendi, author of *How To Be An Antiracist*, cautions, it isn't sufficient to not be a racist; you must actively be an antiracist.

One day, someone will start a post (or whatever the then-current form of popular social media will be) with "Have you always been an antiracist? I wasn't," as they recount their personal story of understanding and then working against racism in America. And that might signal we have turned a corner and made significant improvements toward acknowledging and reducing structural racism and racial inequity.

* * *

*Both Huffman and Williams Bolar broke the law to provide their daughters with what they thought was a better education. Huffman, a white woman, received a sentence of two weeks in jail plus a fine. Williams-Bolar, a Black woman, was initially sentenced to five years in jail. Her sentence was later changed to 10 days and three years' probation.

WHAT DID OCTOBER REVEAL?

By this point in your reading, I hope you see the need for racial justice more clearly and are recognizing that obtaining racial justice will not be, and has not been, easy. You must realize the need, convince others that what is often invisible is real, and then go against years of "it's always been like that" thinking. You must have a racial justice/racial equity lens as a first step to becoming an antiracist.

Sometimes, it is difficult to see how race plays out benignly and destructively in America. Consider this. You're reading a book or a short story. The main character is Amy. You've been reading all about Amy, her life, and her adventures when another character is introduced. You are now told about her Latina neighbor, Mary. Maybe the story moves to her office, where you learn about her African American colleague, Robert. Notice anything? Amy's race hasn't been mentioned. It wasn't necessary because we have all been acculturated to know that Amy is white if race isn't mentioned. White is the standard. White is what is expected. White is the rule. Not always, just most of the time. I offer this observation to prompt you to think about how race can be/should be considered in everything you do. Using the racial lens is a tool that must be cultivated.

There are many racially based expectations and realities in America. Sometimes, just having a racial lens isn't sufficient; it must be a racial *justice* lens. That's why I included "When BIPOC Becomes Camouflage" and "I am My Brother's Keeper." You must ask the right question if you're focused on ensuring that a particular group is included. Be specific in seeking information. Sometimes, the picture is painted with too broad strokes, losing the details. And, sometimes, as in the case of Indigenous People, they aren't even in the picture. They have been treated as a historical footnote, not a current reality.

But my main point in the October collection is that it can happen even when change is a long time coming or seems impossible. Margaret Mead, the anthropologist, said, "Never doubt that a small group of thoughtful, committed citizens can change the world; indeed, it's the only thing that ever has." In the 1850s, a relatively small group of people thought slavery was wrong and worked against it. In the 1950s, a relatively small group thought segregation was wrong and actively worked against it. And, in the 1850s and the 1950s, who could imagine tobacco not being king, one of the money crops that underpinned America's economy? Change can happen. I hope you've decided to actively be a part of the change for racial justice in America.

REFLECT ON THESE QUESTIONS

- Before reading these posts, what was your last thought about Indigenous People in the United States? Why do many think of Indigenous People only in a historical sense?
- What do you think of the term antiracist?

NOTES:

NOVEMBER

Thanksgiving. Dinner table conversations. Security. Home.

Planning for and anticipating Thanksgiving often makes us think of family and home. Many of us were fortunate to have stable, loving families in safe neighborhoods, but not all.

This month's posts are intended to elevate those societal systems that advantage some and disadvantage others. Employment opportunities. The criminal in/justice system. Food. Housing. We take so much for granted. Racial inequity affects many people who aren't as comfortable and privileged as those reading REVEALED.

"But how many people stare inside the body of their nation's racial inequities, their neighborhoods' racial inequities, their occupations' racial inequities, their institutions' racial inequities, and flatly deny that their policies are racist? They flatly deny that racial inequity is a signpost of racist policy. They flatly deny the racist policy as they use racist ideas to justify the racial inequity."
—Ibram X. Kendi, Historian and Author

HOW TO BE AN ANTIRACIST

THE NOURISHMENT OF OUR SOULS

ORIGINALLY PUBLISHED IN APRIL 2020
THE BEGINNING OF THE CORONAVIRUS PANDEMIC.

Once again, restaurateur and chef Jose Andres has shown leadership in the face of calamity. During the pandemic, he was a cover story of Time Magazine. You may recall he set up kitchens in Puerto Rico following Hurricane Maria, in the Bahamas following Hurricane Dorian, and in North and South Carolina following Hurricane Florence. This time, his response is to the coronavirus. Closing his multiple restaurants in DC and elsewhere, he will continue to pay his workers at least for the next few weeks and has set up community kitchens to provide take-out options. And I hear many other restaurant owners are developing creative ways to support their workers and meet community needs.

Food is one of our first thoughts in a disaster.

Like many of you, when the dimensions of this emergency became apparent, I went to the grocery store. I stocked up on everything I needed should I be unable to get to a store for some time. My initial thought was pure survival.

It wasn't hard to get the food I needed. I live less than a half-mile from two chain grocery stores and a farmers' market and within a mile of three additional major grocery stores. Plus, there is a slew of corner stores sprinkled throughout my neighborhood. Food availability is not an issue. Quite a different reality from my neighbors who live in the poorer sections of town, the parts of town with more Black and brown people. Getting to the food they need may not have been as easy. For the poorest sections of my city, there are only three major grocers for the approximately 140,000 people who live there.

'Food Desert' is the term typically used to describe those parts of the city with a dearth of everyday resources, including quality grocery stores. Well, that term fits. A desert is a "barren area where little precipitation occurs, and consequently, living conditions are hostile for plant and animal life." Plant and animal life... hmmm. Sadly, poorer communities often lack the lush greenery of parks seen in more affluent parts of the city. And, if we connect the "lack of precipitation" reference in the definition to the colloquialism, "make it rain," few financial resources come into these communities.

Food Desert is an apt term, but I have been urged to use the term food apartheid. Yes, that works, too, "a policy or system of segregation or discrimination on the grounds of race." The communities I noted above, with only three grocery stores, are 95% African American. These communities, lacking quality, convenient grocery stores, didn't just happen naturally like a desert. They were created. Those in power—who own the stores—decided where their stores would... and would not... be placed.

Consider what happened to my neighborhood 15 years ago. I, along with quite a few neighbors, signed a letter to a major grocery chain requesting a store in our area. Surprisingly, the chain responded and responded quickly but noted that our community did not meet its desired demographic. No dog whistles here. The chain was clear on their reason. Mega gentrification later, that grocery store is now one within a half-mile of my home.

The food story isn't just about convenience. It is about sheer availability. As we face this coronavirus emergency and try to prevent community spread, it is good to hear state and local officials acknowledging the need for food for students as they close schools. They know that far too many children rely on school breakfast and lunch programs as their only meal for the day. The most recent data from the U.S. Department of Agriculture noted about 12% of Americans are food insecure, meaning they don't routinely know where their next meal will come from. But when you disaggregate that data by race, we again see the disparate realities faced by people of color: 22.5% of African American and 18.5% of Latinx households are food insecure.

I find myself cooking comfort foods as I self-quarantine. For me, pot roast is one of those comfort foods, and pot roast just isn't pot roast without potatoes, carrots, and onions. When I peel those onions, I sometimes cry. A chemical in the onions has irritated my tear glands. I can just as easily cry for the inequality many people face daily. Even more so in times like now.

News stories highlight the loss of income for minimum-wage/hourly workers and gig workers not working due to coronavirus-related shutdowns or lessened hours. When was the last time you thought about minimum-wage workers? Do you know what the minimum wage is? How far does a minimum wage worker's paycheck go? As we rely more on grocery store workers, think about their salaries and benefits. So many people who hold the fabric of our society together receive little of our attention or support. As your knowledge grows and you realize the unequal treatment and disparate outcomes, you may experience tears, sadness, or regret.

There's no time for tears; let's not look back with regret. Take action. Let's turn these moments of realization into catalysts for transformation. You have free time now. Google to see where and how you can become an advocate for change.

As I sit down with my pot roast, it's not just a meal providing sustenance; it's comfort food. We must work to fix inadequacies in how things are so they become as they should be for everyone. We must thank and support the stockers in grocery stores, the restaurateurs like Jose Andres, and all who are helping us to get through this situation. It's not just about survival; it's about nourishing our souls.

Lock 'Em Up: The Only Response?

ORIGINALLY PUBLISHED IN NOVEMBER 2022

Late in 2022, I read about a 16-year-old, tried as an adult, who was sentenced to 55 years in prison for two armed carjackings. I was mindlessly scrolling the neighborhood site, Nextdoor, when I saw the post. At first, I thought the incident had happened in Washington, DC, where I live, since there had been a rash of carjackings in my neighborhood. Yet, as I read, I learned this crime had occurred in Louisiana. Louisiana? Why was it posted on my Capitol Hill, DC Nextdoor? Then I noticed the volume of comments and the viciousness of some:

"GOOD and good riddance. Bye-bye!!!!!"

"Good!!! Hope they catch and prosecute more of these carjackers! Teens or not ... people work hard for their cars, and more examples need to be made."

And when someone questioned whether folks were satisfied that the punishment fit the crime, an immediate response was, "Actually, I AM!!!!!" followed by several similar comments and encouragement for DC to be more like Louisiana.

Then, the real impact hit me. This whole situation hurt my soul: another Black child was being lost to the criminal (in)justice system, a system that I know includes a disproportionate number of Black boys and men. I was disturbed that no one seemed to care why this child did this. Lock him away was the only response. No mention of help or rehabilitation. I am not minimizing the crime. He was armed. The carjacking could have resulted in dire consequences (it didn't). I understand those facts. I also know that a 16-year-old is still a child who, according to Stanford University, has almost 10 more years for their brain to fully mature and make wise decisions.

Doing work on racial justice over the last few years has heightened my awareness of how bias, lack of resources and opportunities, and a host of other factors put Black kids at risk and how racism and prejudice are significant, often under-recognized, factors in how "justice" is meted out in America. As I reflected on my reaction to the Nextdoor exchange, I thought back to the viciousness of America's response, not long ago, to drugs and drug-related crimes. Remember "three strikes, you're out," America's response to repeat offenders regardless of the severity of the crime? Now, drug usage has evolved into a public health issue. Growing and selling marijuana has become an acceptable business. Was race a factor in this change? Some suggest that increased drug usage among suburban and rural whites transformed drug usage from a criminal urban problem to a public health problem deserving understanding and treatment. Think about that for a while.

Years ago, a former colleague suggested that prisons should be banned. At the time—about 2017—I couldn't wrap my mind around what I perceived as an incredibly radical and probably unrealistic idea. Now, I am beginning to understand that thinking. When will the social and mental health issues undergird so many behaviors that place people, particularly young people, in prisons be considered? When will society focus on treating those underlying problems as the humane and merited response and consider the caging of humans as radical and reactionary? When will help, not punishment, become the first (or even second) intervention? Does race play a role in preventing this transformation?

For those who know their American history, the 13th Amendment to the U.S. Constitution is correctly reported as the amendment that ended slavery. It is also the amendment that still allows for slavery when a crime is committed. The actual language is:

"Neither slavery nor involuntary servitude, except as a punishment for crime whereof the party shall have been duly convicted, shall exist within the United States, or any place subject to their jurisdiction."

Ava DuVernay's documentary, "*13th,*" and Michelle Alexander's New York Times bestseller, *The New Jim Crow: Mass Incarceration in the Age of Colorblindness,* prompt us to consider the connections between racial injustice and the business of America. Just as slavery offered a financial foundation for this country, today's prison-industrial complex—bail bondsmen, court stenographers, bailiffs, lawyers, judges, prison guards, companies that supply food to prisons, prison security tech companies, and the list goes on—demands a steady increase in what is criminalized and the number who are imprisoned to support the system. And, while African Americans comprise about 14% of America's citizenry, Blacks are about 40% of the incarcerated. Again, just think about that.

A 16-year-old was imprisoned in Louisiana for 55 years, and some people—too many—in a small neighborhood in Washington, DC, cheered.

HOME

ORIGINALLY PUBLISHED IN APRIL 2019

Home. When you say it, what images come to mind? Family? Neighborhood? Playing with your friends as a kid? How does the word make you feel? Content? Happy? Melancholy? Such a small word fills your heart with powerful emotions. Not only does it bring forth memories, but the reality of that place has implications throughout your lifetime.

I think about growing up in the Northside section of Richmond, Virginia. It was a beautiful part of the city with Four Square style houses from the early 1900s, manicured lawns, mature trees, and sidewalks to play hopscotch on. I think of security and peacefulness.

As a kid, I didn't know my parents had secured a part of the American Dream that wasn't available to all. My family was among the first African American families to move into Northside in the early 1950s. Because my parents were moving into a white neighborhood, they could qualify for a bank loan from a white bank. That's right. It wasn't financial capability that made them able to secure a loan with good terms; it was timing.

I hadn't heard of redlining until I was in college. As I recall, it was discussed briefly in an urban sociology class. Neither the professor nor I focused much on it. While the term wasn't coined until the 1960s, the reality of the federal government refusing to insure loans in undesirable areas—literally drawing a red line around neighborhoods on a map—began in the 1930s with the Federal Housing Administration. It wasn't until I heard a presentation by Richard Rothstein, author of *The Color of Law,* that I understood. The federal government had intentionally suppressed the likelihood that African Americans could purchase homes by designating all Black neighborhoods as undesirable. By doing that, the federal government quietly and powerfully said it wouldn't insure loans for home purchases in Black communities.

Now, that didn't mean that Black families couldn't buy homes. In fact, somehow, both sets of my grandparents had purchased homes. It was just more difficult, often with less-than-desirable loan arrangements.

In my grandparents' day, I can only see three options: 1) pay cash—a choice that was very unlikely for most Black people; 2) purchase from an owner by signing a contract, often with a white owner, for payments to be made over 20-30 years. While the loan length was not different from that of a mortgage today, there was a significant risk and potential for swindling. For example, the contract could state that if one payment was late or repairs were not made, the agreement was void, causing the buyer to lose all that had been paid; or 3) secure a loan from a Black-owned bank. The last option was viable, particularly in Richmond. My home city had several Black-owned banks dating back to the late 1880s, but their ability to lend and the conditions of the loans were typically somewhat less desirable than those offered by white-owned banks merely because they had fewer resources.

I suspect that my grandparents, particularly my paternal grandparents, secured a loan from St. Luke Penny Savings Bank, founded by Maggie Walker, a Black woman and the first woman in the United States to charter a bank. She and my grandparents lived in the same neighborhood and knew each other. I can imagine my Father listening, with pride, as my grandparents discussed the importance of saving at Miss Maggie's Bank, as it was called.

It was my Father who taught me the value of owning property. He told me repeatedly that a homeowner could live in his/her home, rent it out in whole or in part, or use it as collateral for a loan when extra money was needed. He understood that a house was far more than a place to live or create memories. It was an investment.

Only in recent years have I come to know that where you live dictates much about the quality of your life. People in African American neighborhoods have shorter lifespans than people in white communities. That difference can be as much as eight years in the Greater Washington, DC area, where I live. Environmental toxins are more prevalent in communities of color. Educational funding and the quality of education are driven largely by local property taxes based on home values. And too many recent incidents have shown the difference in policing practices depending on where you live.

Today, as white people move into Black communities, it is disturbing but perhaps not surprising that the term "gentrifying" is used. The "gentry"—the upper class—has come to the neighborhood, and the community is rising. In my parent's day, Black people moving into a predominately white area was seen as signaling decline. Not much seems to have changed. The underlying narrative remains: black is bad, white is good.

And still, for all of us, home is where the heart is.

Essential Worker Does Not Equal Valued Worker

Originally Published in June 2021

It took the pandemic for many of us to broaden our definition of essential worker and to see that those we tout as "essential" to the functioning backbone of our country are not financially valued.

We compensate many essential workers poorly. They are paid minimum wage, not a livable wage. Today, an employee working 40 hours a week making the federal minimum wage of $7.25/hour earns $15,080 a year. Last year, the National Low Income Housing Coalition reported that minimum wage workers couldn't rent a two-bedroom apartment at market rate in any state in the United States. That's a harsh reality and daily life for many Americans. According to the Economic Policy Institute, perhaps not surprisingly, workers of color are more likely than white workers to earn what they label poverty wages.

The fact that things change but stay the same was driven home to me last month when I took a tour in Colonial Williamsburg.

Like many historical spots in our country, Colonial Williamsburg is trying to better incorporate the lived experience of enslaved people into their representations. So, I was looking forward to a tour titled 'Freedom's Paradox' focused on the institution of slavery in a fledgling nation fighting for freedom. I moved along with the group from one site to another, listening intently to the guides. My ears perked up when the guide portraying one of the landed gentry discussed the provision of food. "Enslaved people in Williamsburg were given two pounds of cornmeal and ½ lb. of meat a week even though they burned about 5000 calories a day working," he told us. I had to do a quick Google search to learn this amount of food equaled about 4500 calories a week for people burning about 30,000 in a typical six-day workweek. A guide portraying an enslaved person continued: "Slaves caught stealing food for themselves or their children were punished severely. Sometimes by a public beating or even by death dependent on how egregious the theft was deemed." That part of the tour concluded by noting that the House of Burgesses, the governing body of the Colony of Virginia, had set the standard of what amount of food should be provided... at a minimum.

Minimum wages.

That's when it struck me: essential workers in the colonial era and those today were and still are paid, in terms of what's needed to exist, to barely survive, certainly not to thrive. Those setting the standards, those governing, then and now, seem to have only nominal regard for people essential to their economic survival. And just as those enslaved in colonial times suffered from malnutrition, poverty wages continue to have a long-term impact. Food deprivation and the reliance on cheap, unhealthy foods have consequences even today, generations later, on the health status of African Americans. Similarly, the inability of many, then and now, to earn a livable wage — in money or in food — leads to a wage theft system with deleterious effects.

While we pay many who provide essential services minimum wage, most of those who shape the country's laws and policies are entirely out of touch with that reality. This was made crystal clear in 1992 when then-President George H. W. Bush, on national television, failed to know the cost of milk during a presidential debate with Bill Clinton and Ross Perot. That incident spotlighted a disconnect, one that still exists between those living ordinary lives and many governing our country. Thirty years later, the nation debates the pros and cons of raising the federal minimum wage to *$15/hour, as many local and state jurisdictions have done, while failing to recognize or acknowledge the impact of poverty wages on our society... and our country.

I wonder what 'essential' means to many of our leaders, not just in government but in commerce, too. When I hear the leaders of Fortune 500 companies proclaim 'Black Lives Matter,' I look to see if they have supported greater benefits for their workers, many of whom are African American, or a $15/hour minimum wage. Rarely do I find that level of commitment. Their bottom line—their profits—not racial equity, is their motivation. Many are "talking the talk" but not "walking the walk." So, while nominally celebrated in media posts, too many essential workers of today are viewed as having minimal value by today's leaders, just as the enslaved people were in the 1700s in Colonial America. Check it out when the next elected official or business leader announces support for racial equity. Minimum wage, minimum value. Let's all support a livable wage for "essential workers" and all workers to thrive, not just survive.

* * *

*In 2023, a proposal was introduced to raise the federal minimum wage to $17/hour by 2028.

WHAT DID NOVEMBER REVEAL?

Here's the final reminder: Addressing racial injustice will take working at those systems that treat one group of people differently than another based on race. We must look deeply at policies and practices in health care, housing, policing, incarceration, education, employment, and every other system that shapes the reality of America.

A few years ago, I read a profound commentary on the need for systemic reform in higher education. It was in the July 26, 2019, issue of the *Chronicle of Higher Education*, written by Patricia McGuire, president of Trinity University. She wrote:

> "Renovation can sometimes cure outmoded structures, but sometimes the only solution is demolition and rebuilding. To make real progress in eliminating the structures of racism that depress the enrollment of black students, universities need to move from gestures of good intentions to real transformation. Rather than using metrics derived from the behaviors of traditional student populations—predominately white, economically secure, attending full time with parental financial support—universities that want to lead real change in eradicating the vestiges of segregation need to develop entirely new approaches to admissions, curricula and pedagogy, support services and measures of academic success that are not seat time in one place."

Everyone isn't the president of a university positioned to recognize and comprehensively address structural or systemic racism. Still, everyone has a position and a voice. Write letters to your local newspaper when you see or hear about racial injustice. Think about how the local newspaper and television stations cover the news. Is there a negative racial bias? If so, let the paper and the stations know you noticed and expect unbiased coverage. Ask questions of your local, state, and national representatives. Their job is to represent all people. Are they doing that job well? Do you see potential areas needing reform to achieve racial justice? Speak up at your church, mosque, synagogue,

PTA meeting, business association, or any board on which you serve. Not once, but repeatedly until you garner allies, gain momentum, and change the situation.

Two more points. You can't solve racism by being nice to people of different races. Courtesy, empathy, and understanding will always be among the hallmarks of a strong community and a great nation, but solving racial injustice takes far more than pleasantries in the grocery store. And, finally, white people, you must take an active role. White people hold the reins of power in every segment of America. For racial justice to happen, white people must understand the role they continue to play in racial injustice, become vocal and active allies in the movement for racial justice, and take the risks that leaders for change must take.

REFLECT ON THESE QUESTIONS

- Did you know what the minimum wage is in your community? If you're not a minimum wage earner, take a minute to approximate what you earn hourly. Can an individual or family thrive in your community earning minimum wage?
- Are you better understanding disproportionate realities faced by people of color? Are you developing a racial equity lens? Try using it the next time you read about a proposal being made in your city or community.

NOTES:

DECEMBER

Holidays. Preparing for the New Year. Reflecting on the Past.

Well, did you do it? Did you read one post a week every week during the past year? Was any new information or different perspectives revealed to you? Did you reflect on them, talk about them with friends or family, and consider the differences between your life and others?

If you haven't done so already, it's time to act, but I hope you've made some changes. Recalibrate.

The last few posts are a reminder of the change you can be.

**"Those who say it can't be done
are usually interrupted by others doing it."
—James Baldwin**

A CHRISTMAS TALE OF NAUGHTY AND NICE

ORIGINALLY PUBLISHED IN DECEMBER 2019

Even though I'm not qualified to advise what stocks to purchase, when to buy, or when to sell, I am making a firm recommendation for what to put in that special Christmas stocking.

NIKE stock.*

That's right.

NIKE stock.

While my knowledge of economics and the stock market is minimal, I know a little about football and a little more about racial equity. So, here's how NIKE, football, and racial equity all come together, tied with a beautiful Christmas bow.

I know the rules of football, can watch a game, and understand what is happening. I even used to follow the Washington DC team but stopped a few years ago. My connection to football, however, did not mean that I knew the names of many of the players. I had never heard of Colin Kaepernick, then quarterback of the San Francisco 49ers, until he decided, in 2016, to kneel during the playing of the National Anthem.

At about that same time, I started my journey to better understand the depth, breadth, and impact of structural racism, racial inequity, and implicit bias. Because I was hyper-attuned to conversations about race and racism—actions and reactions—I focused on what he was doing. Since I was just finding my voice on these topics, I appreciated his use of his NFL quarterback platform to recognize police brutality and oppression against communities of color. From everything I heard him say, he never demeaned the flag or the country. There is no question, however, that his very public action was polarizing. He severed his relationship with his team right before it was rumored he would have been let go. Though a proven talent, no other team approached him. By their inaction, not their words (they have never publicly stated their ban on hiring him), the NFL has blackballed (note the term) Kaepernick. In my view, that's where naughty... and just plain wrong ... came in.

Now, back to NIKE.

In September 2018, two years after Kaepernick's first protest, NIKE did something extraordinary. This multi-national company, focused on sportswear and sports equipment, chose Kaepernick as the face of its "Just Do It" campaign. It was the 30th anniversary of the iconic slogan. Kaepernick had done what the NIKE slogan challenged. He probably didn't consider the many negative consequences of his action, but he wanted to recognize the atrocities happening in America to people who looked like him. He took a stand and suffered the consequences.

In my mind, it was a bold step for NIKE, a major sports company, to go against the general sentiment of the organized sports industry. Football—the NFL—had turned its back on Kaepernick. NIKE, however, had elevated his courage and strength of purpose. The anchor advertising image of the new campaign was a black-and-white photo of Kaepernick emblazoned with the quote, "Believe in something. Even if it means sacrificing everything."

Wow.

Nice... yes, very, very nice.

While I cheered this move by NIKE, its stock price fell immediately, a bad sign in the business world. Boycott NIKE became a Twitter hashtag, and sports teams and athletes around the country announced that they were destroying their NIKE wear. I wanted NIKE to be celebrated. I think they had taken a considerable risk and done the right thing.

I have thought one person can make a difference throughout my adult life. I didn't know what I could do to show my appreciation to NIKE. Then, it occurred to me. I would buy NIKE stock. My purchase certainly would not make a difference like a major investor's, but that wasn't the point. The point was for me to show my appreciation. And I did. On September 10, 2018, I researched how to purchase NIKE shares and the minimum purchase, and then I showed my support for NIKE by buying shares of stock. As I entered the order, sitting at home, alone at my desk, I started to smile. It felt good. NIKE's decision did not have a deleterious impact on the company. In fact, at the time of this posting, the share price has increased by 19% since my initial purchase.

So, if the NIKE logo is emblazoned on your favorite niece or nephew's shoes, shirt, or gym shorts, they might be ripe for learning how the stock market works (economics 101). And since they already demonstrate their support for the company by wearing the products, now would be a great time to discuss how this company used its social consciousness (social justice 101) as you explain why shares of NIKE stock are peeking out of their Christmas stocking.

* * *

*I still own the NIKE stock and am still making a profit.

The Power of One (to Do Good or Bad)

Originally Published in May 2021

Long ago, I was taught not to pay attention to anyone exhibiting racist behavior. "They're powerless," I was told. "Focus instead on the systems that oppress, those societal structures preventing people of color from achieving." And that's what I've done. I've ignored the individuals for years as I examined and discussed structural and systemic racism.

Now, I'm changing my thinking... a bit.

Singly, people exhibiting racist behaviors and shouting racial epithets do have power. They can take my life or that of someone I love because of the color of our skin. Just think of Derek Chauvin and the man in Michigan who shot at a lost Black teen and approached his door to ask for directions. They had power. Or think of those individuals who oversee systems, like local departments of education or land use and zoning commissions. Some have a lethal impact, and others have the power to shape how systems operate. They all have the power to influence.

What is a young child learning when their grandfather uses racist terms or racist tropes when talking about people of color? What are teens and even younger children learning about basic acceptance, or broader celebration, of people who look different from them when they hear messages of racial hatred or racially-charged jokes at the neighborhood barbecue or at the softball game? What are they learning about whom to fear, who to trust, who is smart, and who is lazy? What stereotypes are being reinforced? What values are being shaped? I'm talking about what is often referred to as observational learning or role modeling. The words and behaviors of adults have a powerful impact on the children and young people in their lives.

Our families, neighbors, teachers, and the many adults who form our community's fabric shape who we are. They do so by what they do and say... and what they don't do or don't say. What situations are not discussed around your kitchen table? As the trial of Derek Chauvin unfolded on television and in newspapers, did your teenage children—who were bound to hear something about it—know what you felt about the incident and the verdict? Do they know what you think as an increasing number of Asian Americans are assaulted? Incidents that happen in the light of day. Watched with inaction, or perhaps helplessness, or even guilt.

Racist ideas are seeded by the adults in young people's lives, by those who believe in a racial hierarchy that places white people at the top of humanity. Those adults nurture and develop the notions, the seeds that they plant. Sadly, the sin of omission also shapes values by what isn't said or done by adults who claim they are liberal, unbiased, and non-racist.

A single person can be the spark that ignites the flame of racial injustice or lights the way for others to fight for change. Each of us decides what imprint we will leave in the world.

I can no longer minimize the power of racist individuals.

The Greatest Generation

Originally Published in July 2021

In 1998, journalist Tom Brokaw coined: "The Greatest Generation." It was the title of his book on ordinary Americans who, during and after World War II, were such an important part of this country's growth and success. Many celebrated his stories using words like courage, sacrifice, and honor to describe the valor and contributions of everyday people. While Brokaw's book wasn't only about veterans, World War II formed the core of his greatest generation.

For me, there's another complement of "greatest generation" heroes. War veteran isn't their primary identity, even though many may have had a connection to that or the previous war. In fact, the segregation of troops made them, and their children, even more aware of how America was failing Black people. My greatest generation is the 1950s and '60s, unarmed, nonviolent marchers of the Civil Rights movement. Their enemy wasn't tyranny from a foreign country but the oppression of Americans, by Americans, right here at home. They, too, are aptly described by the words "courage, sacrifice, and honor."

My greatest generation includes people like Carolyn Wilson and Dorothy Batson, elders I recently heard talk about their experiences in a little-known but horrific event in Danville, Virginia—Bloody Monday, June 10, 1963. They had marched to the courthouse steps, protesting segregation and racial inequality. To break up the demonstration, police turned high-pressure water hoses on them. The power of the hoses knocked Ms. Batson down the steps. For the other marchers on the street, the aim and force of the water, combined with the street's incline, pushed them down and under parked cars, adding to their injuries. Ms. Wilson and Ms. Batson told the audience that white bus drivers and garbage workers were deputized, armed with nightsticks, and given the authority to beat them. Ms. Batson reminded the audience that, due to the norms of the time, women and girls didn't wear pants then, only skirts and dresses, sharing how the gravel and concrete from the streets dug into their exposed legs as the water carried them along—a little told fact that adds to the physical pain suffered by female protesters. The small audience listening to them was transfixed as these women calmly told their story of actively participating in a movement to gain rights that America had promised to all but only delivered to some.

As I, a Black woman, listened to them, I wondered if I could have done what they did. Could I have gone into a situation where I knew I would most likely be harmed, possibly killed, to fight for my rights? Just as I started to think if I had the guts, Ms. Wilson reminded the audience that they weren't courageous, just teens and young adults who probably viewed themselves, unconsciously, as invincible. Ms. Batson agreed that as a 20-year-old, she doesn't remember being afraid, just tired of "not being treated as people." Surely, their age contributed to their decision to join the march, but it wasn't bravado. It was bravery. They knew the members of the KKK in their town who met boldly and openly. They definitely knew there would be repercussions. That's what makes their actions great—moving forward, marching even though armed haters lined the street, poised and probably anxious to attack.

Whenever Brokaw's greatest generation is discussed, the commentator will say something like, "We're losing over 350 of these heroes every day," simply acknowledging their aging and life's passage. Almost 60 years after it occurred, I happened to be in a room listening to Ms. Wilson and Ms. Batson tell of an incident I'd never heard of, even though I grew up only 150 miles away. So many stories in your own town or very nearby are unknown. There are far too many unrecognized heroes or leaders whose role in the movement has been forgotten. Seek them out, learn their stories, and celebrate their leadership. There isn't much time left.

For me, "the greatest generation" will always be those men, women, and children who marched, were beaten, jailed, and, sometimes, killed so that I might have the rights I do today. As a country, we have much further to go to achieve racial justice, but I—we—owe a huge debt to those who paved the way.

A Room with A View ... Point

ORIGINALLY PUBLISHED IN MAY 2023

Several weeks ago, I attended a presentation held at a private club in Washington, DC. I was looking forward to the topic, "Alleviating Poverty: The Universal Basic Income Approach." One of the speakers was a colleague from a monthly breakfast group I've been a part of for over a decade. In fact, I was so looking forward to the presentation that I hadn't paid much attention to the location.

That changed as soon as I walked into the room. I had been to this club before but saw it differently this time for some reason. I was struck immediately by its grandeur. Versailles came to mind. It was ornate, with gold leaf, many mirrors, and corner cherubs. The place settings sparkled, ready for us to enjoy dinner before the presentation.

It was breathtaking, and it made me uncomfortable.

Was this where we should be discussing alleviating poverty?

My discomfort wasn't just about the physical environment. It was the combination of the setting and the attendees.

The people in this room were members of the club, literally and figuratively, and their guests. There was lots of chatting during the cocktail hour before the event. One person commented to me that she had been married in this room. The venue was familiar and comfortable for them. They were proud of it. They repeatedly celebrated the quality of the food, the comfort of the club's library, and the proficiency and long tenure of the staff. This was their place. They were at home.

I had expected the attendees to be older and white. I just hadn't thought I'd be the only Black participant. I'm pretty sure everyone was white except for three of the five presenters, a staffer accompanying one of the speakers, and me. So, was that why I was uncomfortable? Was this about race? I don't think so. The dissonance, I felt, was more about class and understanding/frame of reference.

To me, these were wealthy people. Their conversation, however, suggested they considered themselves in the middle class. Educated? Yes, but other than that, I think they thought of themselves as Joe and Susie Average. A frame of reference is everything, right? Had anyone in the room ever been poor or had direct familial relationships or contact via deep friendship with poor people? Could they understand poverty?

Several people commented that many in the club were liberals and that all were knowledge seekers. Liberals? Was this said so I'd think they were proponents of racial justice and knowledgeable about racial injustice? Was it code? Knowledge seekers? I knew that learning was one of the founding principles of the club. Was this presentation primarily an intellectual opportunity to understand the concept of universal basic income? Did they think that a universal basic income would level the racial playing field, not considering the depth, breadth, and impact of structural racism? Was I overthinking this? So much swirled through my head as I sat in that room. Did anyone else feel the disconnect?

For those of us who see ourselves as change agents, we are the bridge between the community most impacted by the problem to be addressed and the community that, by their positions and power, hold some of the keys to addressing those problems. We must be comfortable in both places, going to both to gain and provide information and to discuss strategy. We—the change agents—must be able to navigate very wealthy/powerful/white spaces and translate the realities of poverty to people with little experience (which the panel of presenters did brilliantly).

My concerns about what people did and didn't know about race, racism, poverty, and class didn't need to be addressed in one evening. I needed to move beyond the setting and focus on the potential. Because of the inequities of our society, the people in this room had the required financial, social, and political resources to respond.

Was this private club in Washington, DC, the right setting for a conversation on universal basic income? I think it was one of many "right" venues. The club's program committee had recommended the topic. The attendees were a ready, willing, and able group, so let the education begin. Plus, the right people are always the ones in the room, right? Still, what a room....

White People, There Is so Much to Gain

Originally Published in December 2020

If you're reading my blog, you're probably among those fighting for racial justice, some at the macro-level of societal transformation, others working for enhanced understanding among family. Or maybe you're just beginning to recognize and reflect on racial injustice's depth, breadth, and impact.

Regardless, here is my question. What drives you: wanting the oppressed to have a greater opportunity or to free the oppressor? To my white readers, I want to call this out: True racial equity will bring significant benefits ... to you.

You're accustomed to hearing racial justice advocates speak of the needs of the oppressed: lost opportunities, lost potential, and a focus on 'lesser than' statistics, such as home ownership or educational outcomes. Tangible data is compared across races. And by that data, the white population is better off than communities of color on multiple fronts. Because of this, the racial equity battle often focuses solely on gains needed for the oppressed.

But, white people, have you ever reflected on what you will gain?

First, your own psychological well-being. You have to believe, to some degree, that Black and brown people are more criminal or less enterprising, for example, to accept their overrepresentation in prisons and underrepresentation in places of academic and financial success. Noted author and activist James Baldwin suggested that white America needs to believe in Black pathology to justify what has been, and continues to be, done and to alleviate any obligation to fix the problem. Yes? No? Is there cognitive dissonance, a disconnect between what you say you believe (everybody has a fair chance) and what is the allowed reality in America?

Now to history. What has been lost to white people by not fully understanding our country's history? As more comprehensive explanations of historical 'facts' are revealed, are you looking more critically at your heroes, at the foundation of America? Are you considering what/who supported your ancestors' or immediate forbearers' ability to pull themselves up by their bootstraps? Did they really do that? "Pull themselves up by their bootstraps," I mean? No supportive government programs? Think about the GI Bill, preferential housing, or unconstrained banking policies. No help from families or social networks better positioned to offer support? How is your authentic sense of self affected? Is there some internal alignment that needs to happen to make your worldview/familial context more coherent with truth?

Then, just one more thing. Much attention has been given to the value of diversity in the workplace. Problem-solving, research has shown, benefits from different viewpoints and people with varying life experiences. Varied thinking and cultures are enriching, not limiting. If this is true in the workplace, why would it be different in friendship groups or neighborhoods? What is missed by having racial homogeneity in so many parts of your life?

The balance of assets and societal power is unequal. That is true, but adjusting that imbalance doesn't make anyone a loser. Everyone wins. We all win if fewer resources are used, for example, to imprison, freeing up more to support asset building, the true provision of quality education for all, clean water everywhere, or medical research. Who loses if more Black or brown people can purchase homes, building their wealth and ability to contribute even more to our country's economic viability?

I know there is an intangible benefit to resolving the internal moral or psychological battle among some in the white community. There is significant inherent value in embracing the humanity and worth of all people. And there is tangible value to more people contributing to the common good.

As I write this, I realize I struggle to find the right words. I can't make the case as eloquently as I would like. Still, I know that the deficit model of fighting for racial equity is neither the whole story nor the best strategy. Self-interest is a powerful motivator. You must fight for racial equity to benefit the oppressor and the oppressed.

WHAT DID DECEMBER REVEAL

If you haven't started already, now it's time to recalibrate. It's time to make adjustments in the way you live and act based on new information, new experiences, or simply new insights realized after deep reflection. It was that process of learning and reflecting that led me to stop smoking decades ago and deep reflection that caused me to realize that one person can make a tremendous difference for good or for evil. The rippling out of impact is real.

I still believe in Dr. Martin Luther King's words. I, too, want my children (and grandchildren) to be judged by the content of their character, not the color of their skin... the texture/style of their hair, their name, where they were educated, or the zip code that follows their address. I want my children and grandchildren to live happy and fulfilled lives driven by their desires, not societal limitations.

I believe that the person who has the cure for diseases that challenge us may be living in a zip code without encouraging teachers in the school or well-equipped science labs. I believe that the person who can address the climate challenges facing us just had their job application denied because their name suggested to the decision-makers that they wouldn't fit in. And I believe that the person who can bring together our divided political reality won't get that job that will position them to be a change agent because they didn't attend the Ivy League school attended by most of the organization's current partners. Bias, prejudice, and racist policies are real, and they are holding all of us back.

I'm asking that you be that one person, that advocate for change, working for a more racially just world wherever you sit. It won't be easy, but what have you ever achieved that is truly meaningful that came easily? Every success/accomplishment involved study, more study, coaching, testing, then repeat, repeat, repeat. What I'm asking is for you to believe that the goal of racial justice is worth the challenge, the hardships that may occur, and the bumps and crevasses in the road.

The December posts were intended to show you the power that you possess and to remind you that addressing racial inequity is a win-win for all of us. For centuries, we have been told, directly or indirectly, that someone must lose—typically white people—for other races and ethnicities to gain their piece of the American dream. Let me offer one final reading recommendation. Written by Heather McGee, an expert in social and economic policy, *The Sum of Us: What Racism Costs Everyone And How We Can Prosper Together* will offer new perspectives on how we came to believe in the shrinking pie and why it's not shrinking but growing.

You did it. You started your racial equity learning journey. Now, how does the learning continue?

REFLECT ON THESE QUESTIONS

- What was the last injustice that prompted you to take a stand? What did you risk? Did the injustice affect your family, or was it beyond your family?
- When your children and grandchildren look back on your life, will they know what was important enough for you to take a stand? Will racial justice be on that list?

NOTES:

Conclusion

Thank you.

For months, I couldn't think of how to end REVEALED. Nothing seemed quite right. Then, I thought, what else? I should finish it with a blog post and a thank you.

Thank You is Enough

ORIGINALLY PUBLISHED IN JANUARY 2020

The sidewalks in the neighborhood were narrow and uneven. People walking in opposite directions often had to shift or even stop to pass without bumping into each other. In this century-plus old section of the city, there were many tree roots twisting beneath the brick sidewalks, creating tilts and ridges that threatened each step. So, the need to pay attention to where you were walking was necessary and the norm.

The first time, I wasn't sure he was who I thought he was.

For about a month, I would pass him every day around 7:45 a.m. after dropping my son—AJ—off at preschool. As I walked to the metro, mentally moving from mom to nonprofit exec, I would think about what I had to do at work that day. I was still adjusting to taking AJ to preschool. Until that September, he had been at home with a care provider. Now, it was time to get him into a group with other children. So, I had to get him up, dressed, and fed... and me, too. As the saying goes, "it" — parenthood, in this case — "was more than a notion." In my early 40s, I was an older mother, and the adjustments to motherhood had been many as I also worked to succeed in my career. Some mornings were a bit unfocused as life's demands jostled through my mind. Not paying careful attention, I had almost tripped on the sidewalk the previous week. On that first morning, when I saw him, I was head down, focused on carefully negotiating the uneven bricks. I glanced up just as I passed him. The glimpse was quick, perfunctory. I wasn't sure it was him, but I thought it was.

On the next day and the subsequent days when we passed, I was sure. I knew who he was. At first, I would nod and smile. Then, after a few days, I started to say, "Good morning, sir." To which he would nod and smile, sometimes replying with a pleasant "Good morning."

At no time during those few weeks in 1997, when our paths crossed every morning, did I ever try to have a conversation with Congressman John Lewis. I wish I had.

I was reminded of those small encounters when I heard the announcement of his stage 4 pancreatic cancer.

When Congressman Elijah Cummings, a long-time Civil Rights champion, passed last October, Speaker of the House Nancy Pelosi referred to him as Congress' North Star. I understood why. He was a strong and outspoken advocate for what was morally right. But John Lewis has always been my North Star. In 1997, I wouldn't have thought of him with that term, but I have always admired his courage. I knew of his Civil Rights work, particularly the march across the Edmund Pettus Bridge. For me, he was then, and still is, the personification of fierce leadership and dedication to purpose.

After reading his memoir, Walking With The Wind, in 1998, the year after our brief encounters, I remember wishing I had engaged him as we passed each other. His leadership was even deeper and more critical to the Civil Rights movement than I had initially known. But what would I possibly have said to him or asked? How would I have broached meaningful topics in those brief moments? He was hurrying to important committee meetings, I suspect, with no time to carry on a conversation. I do, however, remember wishing I had said, "Thank you" as we passed on that sidewalk.

I was fortunate. I had a chance to say just that almost twenty years later.

In 2016, he and then-Congressman Sam Johnson of Texas were presented with the Congressional Patriot Award by the Bipartisan Policy Center. I was lucky enough to be invited to the event held at the Library of Congress. I brought my copy of Walking With The Wind, knowing I would ask him to sign it if the circumstance presented itself. As the guests mingled in an ornately beautiful room before the ceremony, I saw him enter without fanfare. I gathered my courage, walked up to him, and thanked him for all he had done for me, for people who looked like me, and for our country. Graciously, he thanked me for the kind words and signed my book.

It wasn't until 2016 that I started to get into good trouble.

Throughout my life, I've had interesting jobs that I thought made a difference – jobs that were working to improve the quality of life for some who were neglected or forgotten. Good jobs. Impactful positions. But I never felt that I was living my purpose, not until 2016. It was then that I began curating "Putting Racism on the Table" for the Washington Regional Association of Grantmakers (WRAG). This was a learning series exploring race and racism, with members of philanthropy in the District of Columbia, suburban Maryland, and Northern Virginia as the primary audience. That was when I started to better understand racial injustice. I knew that I wanted to help others see it, to think about racial injustice, and to work for racial justice. My mantra became REVEAL, REFLECT, RECALIBRATE.

Thank you to john a. powell (lack of capitalization is his preference), Robin DiAngelo, Julie Nelson, Manuel Pastor, James Bell, and Gail Christopher. These were the first experts in WRAG's series, "Putting Racism on the Table." They, along with Ibram X. Kendi, Lonnie Bunch, David Williams, Inca Mohamed, Yanique Redwood, Nat Williams, Hanh Le, and Rick Moyers, were all part of the village that helped to crystallize my thinking about racial injustice and the path to racial justice. And, the martyrs—Trayvon Martin, Tamir Rice, Ahmaud Arbery, Elijah McClain, Breonna Taylor, George Floyd, and many others—those whose deaths truly hurt my soul while uplifting me to live more in my purpose and give meaning to their lives and deaths.

Thank you to those who followed my blog, *Daughters of the Dream*, and sent encouraging messages noting how I had opened their eyes or explained a racial reality in a way that they could see it. And to those who shared with me what they were doing to fight racial injustice. Thank you to my former WRAG colleague Rebekah Seder, a strong racial justice ally with an astute eye for organizing and editing. And thank you to Dennis Lowery and the Adducent team for believing in the importance of this work.

And, of course, thank you to my close friends and family – Janice Bowie, Cassandra Joubert, Linda Bowen, Cheryl Clarke, Joyce Soria, Nicki, and AJ for always being supportive and encouraging.

I hope REVEALED has started or contributed to your lifelong journey to understand racial injustice and to fight for justice.

> **"Ours is not the struggle of one day, one week, or one year. Ours is not the struggle of one judicial appointment or presidential term. Ours is the struggle of a lifetime, or maybe even many lifetimes, and each one of us in every generation must do our part."**
> **–John Lewis**

209

Milton Keynes UK
Ingram Content Group UK Ltd.
UKHW020924231123
433129UK00016B/1016